The Art of Abstracting

The Art of Abstracting

Second Edition

Edward T. Cremmins

 INFORMATION RESOURCES PRESS

First edition © 1982 by ISI Press.

Available from
Information Resources Press
1110 North Glebe Road
Suite 550
Arlington, Virginia 22201

Library of Congress Catalog Card Number 95-82341

ISBN 0-87815-066-8

To Karla

ABSTRACT

A three-stage analytical reading method is described for the writing of informative and indicative abstracts by authors and documental information processing abstractors. Good reading, thinking, writing, editing, and revising skills are required for good abstracts. Adhering to abstracting rules and conventions and maintaining cooperative professional relationships also contribute to the preparation of high-quality abstracts.

Contents

Figures

Preface

What has any poet to trust more than the feel of the thing? Theory concerns him only until he picks up his pen, and it begins to concern him again as soon as he lays it down. But when the pen is in his hand he has to write by itch and twitch, though certainly his itch and twitch are intimately conditioned by all his past itching and twitching, and by all his past theorizing about them. (p. 288)

—JOHN CIARDI (1963)

On April 1st, 1986, as I read the above extract of the late poet John Ciardi's words, quoted in his obituary in *The New York Times,* it had been about five years since I had put down my own pen after finishing the long spell of nonpoetic itching and twitching and theorizing that was required for writing the first edition of this guidebook on the writing, editing, and revising of abstracts.

Now, about nine years later, I have picked up my pen again, to itch and twitch over some past and present theorizing about the themes in the first edition of this book and some new, related ones that have since come to mind.

Many minor and a few major revisions have been made to most of the original chapters. New chapters have been added on the adding of value and making of meaning during documental information processing, the editing and revising of author abstracts and computational (machine or automated) abstracts, and the thought processes that are used during documental information processing. In essence, value is added to the draft version of the abstract when the abstractor reviews it to ensure that a diverse amount of information has been coherently included within an intrinsically unified structure. The abstractor then attempts to make more meaning by rapidly comparing this version of the abstract against the text of the material being abstracted to determine whether he or she can add still more meaningful information in the final version.

The literature on abstracting has been thoroughly reviewed, extracted, or cited where appropriate. Also, a survey is appended of the literature on other forms of summarization and the relationship between abstracting and summarizing (see Appendix 5).

The suggested three-stage reading model for abstracting that was introduced in the first edition has been revised and expanded as follows:

Stage	Old Name	New Name
I	Retrieval Reading	Exploratory-to-Retrieval Reading (Part II, Chapters 5 and 6)
II	Creative Reading	Responsive-to-Inventive Reading (Part III, Chapters 7 to 9)
III	Critical Reading	Connective (Value-to-Meaning) Reading (Part IV, Chapters 10 to 13)

When reading for abstracting, one should first *explore* the material to identify candidate information for *retrieval* (Stage I); then *respond,* not react, to the candidate information and *inventively synthesize* the most relevant portions into a draft abstract (Stage II); and, finally, carefully review the draft to add *value* to and make more *meaning* of it (Stage III). These changes to the reading scheme for abstracting are a result of 14 further years of research and the testing, refining, using, and teaching of the concepts described in the first edition.

One theme of this book holds that the development and maintenance of cooperative professional relationships between abstractors, editors, managers, sponsors of abstracting services, and users of abstracts are vital to the composition of well-construed abstracts. Similar personal cooperative relationships have been vital to the composition of this book. I am deeply indebted to Ben Weil, who reviewed two versions of the manuscript for the first edition and offered numerous cogent suggestions on how to make it less indicative and more informative and instructive. For the second edition, Saul Herner was an equally essential mentor.

Others to whom I am deeply indebted for their encouragement and worthwhile suggestions during the preparation of the second edition are James Whang, Rodney Savage, Brad Hilton, F. Scott Truesdale, Trudi

Bellardo Hahn, David Battey, Isaac Welt, Suzanne Humphrey, Brigitte Endres-Niggemeyer, Stella Koppel, Kerming Tsaur, and Ming Chang.

William Wilson and his staff once again furnished reference guidance and full access to research materials in the collection of the College of Library and Information Services Library at the University of Maryland in College Park, Maryland.

Finally, I owe a deep debt to Gene Allen, whose editing greatly enhanced the content, flow, and clarity of the manuscript.

PART I

ABSTRACTS AND ABSTRACTING

INDICATIVE ABSTRACT

The functional and creative writing characteristics of abstracting are discussed. The types of published materials that are abstracted are described, as well as the content and types of abstracts. Also mentioned are the purpose of abstracts and their value to readers, authors, primary publishers and editors, information processing abstractors and indexers, information retrieval specialists, students, and teachers. The importance of analytical reading in the writing of quality abstracts is discussed.

CHAPTER 1

About Abstracting

Abstracting may be defined as the process of eliminating unnecessary detail to reveal underlying order, pattern, structure or some other characteristic that is otherwise not obvious, or that is so obvious as to be overlooked. The process of abstracting is the same whether a person abstracts a book or article into a paragraph summary, treats a grasshopper as an abstract mechanical object composed of a mass suspended on levers and springs in order to analyze its locomotion, or creates an abstract painting of the female figure that reveals unsuspected visual relationships. (p. 87)

—ROBERT S. ROOT-BERNSTEIN (1991)

WHAT IS AN ABSTRACT

Within the scientific and technical literature, particularly that on library and information science, education, communication, and technical writing, answers to the question "What is an abstract?" are as varied in length and content as the actual abstracts that are published in different abstract journals. The American National Standards Institute's (ANSI, 1979) definition is one of the most terse: "An abstract is an abbreviated, accurate representation of the contents of a document, preferably prepared by its author(s) for publication with it. Such abstracts are also useful in access publications and machine-readable data bases." (p. i)

Well-written abstracts are highly structured, concise, and coherent, and are the result of a thorough analysis of the content of the abstracted

3

materials. Abstracts may be more readable than the basic documents, but because of size constraints, they rarely equal and never surpass their information content.

Well-written abstracts have been described by Ashworth (1973) as the product of the highest craftsmanship:

> To take an original article, understand it and pack it neatly into a nutshell without loss of substance or clarity presents a challenge which many have felt worth taking up for the joys of achievement alone. These are the characteristics of an art form. (p. 46)

The art of abstracting demands the application of extensive reading, thinking, writing, editing, and revising skills (discussed in detail in Parts II through V of this text). The remainder of Part I presents additional background information on the abstracting process.

WHAT IS ABSTRACTED

Publishers of primary journals furnish abstracts with most articles on theoretical or experimental research themes that are contained in a given issue. These publishers normally do not provide abstracts of editorial material, short communications, or letters to the editor.

"Access" (abstracting and indexing) publishers (see "access abstracts" in the appended Glossary) either publish collections of abstracts in abstract journals or maintain them in files that now generally are stored in computer memories or on compact disks for retrieval on demand. In addition to comprehensive coverage of the items that are abstracted in relevant primary journals, access publishers also selectively abstract books, editorials, patents, research progress reports, conference proceedings, and letters to the editors of scientific, technical, and scholarly publications that contain substantive information of lasting value. Some access publishers also abstract the information contained in such nonprint materials as filmstrips, cassette tapes, and visual aids.

PURPOSE AND VALUE OF ABSTRACTS

Abstracts assist readers in deciding whether they should consult the full text of the abstracted material by providing them with more information than that given in the title, annotation, or index terms. As McArthur

(1992) has stated, "After reading the abstract, someone may decide to read the whole document or (in the case of a public presentation) attend the meeting at which the document will be read out and/or discussed." (p. 7)

Lancaster (1991) also points out the value of translated abstracts and the current awareness value of all abstracts:

> Abstracts are particularly useful in illuminating the content of items written in languages unfamiliar to a particular reader. . . . The printing and distribution of abstracts is effective in keeping people informed of newly published literature in their fields of interest (i.e., providing for current awareness). (p. 89)

Cleveland and Cleveland (1990), who note that the first abstract journal was published in 1665, state that "Abstracts are written to decrease the time and effort it takes to search the overwhelming output from research and scholarship around the world." (p. 6)

Besides their primary value to readers of scholarly, technical, and scientific monographs and journals, abstracts are also important to authors, primary journal publishers and editors, professional abstractors, other information processing and retrieval specialists, and students and faculty taking or teaching library and information science or technical writing courses. When authors write their own abstracts, they can further evaluate the style and content of their research papers or monographs and identify and correct shortcomings.

Author abstracts that accompany manuscripts submitted for publication can ease the selection process for the editorial staffs of primary journal publishers. Staff editors can use the abstracts to estimate the depth of treatment and degree of originality of the material. The information in the abstract may even indicate those portions of the text that need to be expanded, clarified, or eliminated. Author abstracts also can be used as a primary source of ideas for promoting the journals or conference proceedings in which they are published.

Professionals who abstract documents that have been published without an abstract or who revise author-written abstracts to conform to the specifications of alerting or information retrieval systems can earn substantial income if they are proficient and highly productive. Subject specialists or volunteer abstractors who write abstracts as an avocation can benefit by keeping abreast of advances in their fields of interest. Other information processing and retrieval specialists, such as indexers, search analysts, and lexicographers, use abstracts to assist them in their indexing, retrieval, and vocabulary control tasks, respectively.

Rowley (1988) points out that the learning of abstracting skills aids students in performing intellectual tasks both on and off campus:

> But even the student who has no intention of entering the sector of the profession that is responsible for the production of abstracts will find abstracting skills valuable. They can help in effective note-taking, digestion of current literature, analysis of committee papers and the presentation of reports. The efficient analysis of professional and technical documents is an asset in many spheres of activity. . . . (p. 11)

Similar benefits accrue to faculty members and others who give instruction in the writing of abstracts but do not necessarily write them in volume themselves.

TYPES OF ABSTRACTS

Abstracts often are classified on the basis of content, purpose, and structure, as well as authorship. Abstracts of articles in primary journals are usually called *author abstracts*, although some are written by subject specialists or members of the editorial staff of the publishing house. Abstracts written for access publications and services typically are composed by subject or information specialists. In this text, these manually written abstracts will be referred to as "documental information processing abstracts" or "information processing abstracts," as opposed to those that are produced by programmed computers (which will be designated as "computational abstracts," discussed in Chapter 16).

Author and information processing abstracts may be further classified according to purpose, structure, content, and method of preparation. Within this classification scheme, the two most common types are *informative* and *indicative* (*descriptive*) abstracts, which will be discussed in the last section of this chapter. Other types include *modular* and *critical* abstracts (see Glossary).

CONTENT OF ABSTRACTS

Abstracts generally contain up to four, usually sequential, information elements that describe or extract information from the basic document. As described in the *American National Standard for Writing Abstracts* (ANSI, 1979), these elements state "the purpose, methodology, results, and conclusions presented in the original document." (p. i) Methods for preparing this type of abstract generally will be discussed in this book. A *findings-oriented* abstract, in which the most important results or conclusions are placed first, followed by supporting details, other findings, and methodology, is also mentioned in the *American National Standard for Writing Abstracts*.

Once authors or information processing abstractors acquire a good understanding of the procedures for writing the more conventional types of abstracts, they should have no difficulty in writing findings-oriented abstracts or other types that use variations in format.

When examples of abstracts are discussed in the following pages of this book, the four information elements are referred to by slightly different terms. These are (1) the primary "aboutness" element (information on purpose, scope, and methodology comprising the first sentence); (2) the secondary aboutness element (those sentences that follow the first sentence, if any, that contain additional information on purpose, scope, and methodology); (3) the results or findings; and (4) the conclusions and/or recommendations.

INDICATIVE AND INFORMATIVE ABSTRACTS

Indicative (descriptive) and informative abstracts are defined variously in the literature. Many definitions suggest that an informative abstract should be a miniature version of the full paper, whereas an indicative abstract should resemble a table of contents.

For ease of instruction, this text will consider indicative abstracts to be those that contain information on the purpose, scope, or methodology, but not the results or findings, conclusions, or recommendations. An example of this type of abstract is given in Figure 1. Also, each part of this book is introduced with an indicative abstract.

Progress in modeling human cognitive processes is reviewed, emphasizing the use of computer programming languages as a formalism for modeling and computer simulation of the behavior of the systems modeled. Elementary and higher processes are examined, and neural models are briefly described.

Figure 1   Indicative abstract. SOURCE: **Adapted from the abstract in Simon (1981, p. 364).**

The preferred definition for an informative abstract in this text is that although it may contain information on purpose, scope, and methods, it must also contain information on results or findings, conclusions, or recommendations. Figure 2 shows an informative abstract that contains all four information elements. In Figure 3, the indicative abstract given in Figure 1 has been expanded into a combined "indicative–informative" abstract by the addition of a conclusion.

The embryotoxicity of hexachlorocyclopentadiene was studied in mice and rabbits. Pregnant animals were given 5, 25, or 75 mg/kg per day by gavage on days 6 to 15 (mice) or days 6 to 18 (rabbits) of gestation. Food and water consumption and weight were recorded daily. Mice and rabbit dams were killed on days 18 and 29 of gestation, respectively. Fetuses were removed and examined for malformations. Fertility of the treated mice and rabbits was not significantly different from that of control animals. The dose of 75 mg/kg per day was toxic to rabbit dams; no toxic effects were seen in mice at any dose. No significant effects on the average number of implantations, live fetuses, or resorptions were observed in either species.

Figure 2   Informative abstract. Not published previously.

Progress in modeling human cognitive processes is reviewed, emphasizing the use of computer programming languages as a formalism for modeling and computer simulation of the behavior of the systems modeled. Elementary and higher processes are examined, and neural models are briefly described. Theories of human cognitive processes can be attempted at the level of neural, elementary information (retrieval from memory, scanning down lists in memory, comparing simple symbols), or higher information processes (problem solving, concept attainment).

Figure 3   Indicative–informative version of the indicative abstract in Figure 1.

CHAPTER 2

Informative Words for Authors of Abstracts

There are four things that make this world go round: love, energy, materials, and information. We see about us a critical shortage of the first commodity, a near-critical shortage of the second, increasing shortage of the third, but an absolute glut of the fourth. (p. ix)

—ROBERT A. DAY (1983)

In the preface to his book, *How to Write and Publish a Scientific Paper,* Day (1983) uses the four words *love, energy, materials*, and *information* to underscore his general advice to authors of scientific papers before he presents more specific advice, not only on the writing of a scientific paper, but also on writing review papers, conference reports, and theses. Continuing his preface, Day advises authors on how to alleviate the problem of the glut of information:

> We in science, of necessity, must contribute to the glut. But let us do it with love, especially love of the English language, which is the cornerstone of our intellectual heritage; let us do it with energy, the energy we need to put into the scientific paper so that the reader will not need to use much energy to get the information out of the paper; and let us husband our materials, especially our words, so that we do not waste inordinate quantities of paper and ink in trying to tell the world more than we know. (p. ix)

11

That which is appropriate for the writing of all other components of a scientific, technical, or scholarly paper is also appropriate for the writing of the abstract by its author or authors.

In the remainder of this chapter, Day's advice for writers of scientific papers on the four things that he feels make the world go round (love, energy, materials, and information) will be elaborated on for authors of abstracts under three headings: using second-wind *love* and *energy*, reducing *information*, and handling *materials*. Then, two other elements, *value* and *meaning*, that are also important to the writing of good abstracts will be discussed under the headings "adding *value*" and "making *meaning*."

USING SECOND-WIND LOVE AND ENERGY

> Everyone knows what it is to start a piece of work, either intellectual or muscular, feeling stale—or *oold*, as an Adirondack guide once put it to me. And everybody knows what it is to "warm up" to his job. The process of warming up gets particularly striking in the phenomenon known as "second wind." (James, 1947, p. 40)

The original or revised version of the paper is almost complete. The author has invested far more love, energy, and time in thinking through his or her ideas, researching them, testing them, and writing them into manuscript form than was ever imagined when he or she first decided to share them through publication.

The paper now has unity and coherence, and the ideas flow well from the introduction to the conclusions and recommendations; footnotes are numbered, verified, and in proper sequence; and all references are in accordance with the specifications of the publisher to whom the manuscript is being submitted. One of the final steps remaining before submission of the full manuscript for refereeing, review, or acceptance is to prepare or revise the abstract.

This seems simple enough. Besides a few minor style conventions on verb usage, symbols, and abbreviations, the instructions for the particular abstract might ask only for an "informative abstract of about 150 words." This appears to pose no major problem, even though the author now may be feeling intellectually "stale—or *oold*," as James (1947) put it in his essay on "The Energies of Men." But if the author does not have a firm grasp of the fundamentals of preparing an informative abstract, this request definitely could pose a major problem—one that could well require a substantial burst of "second-wind" love and energy to ensure that the completed abstract approximates the diversity of information and unity of structure of the full text of the paper.

REDUCING INFORMATION

> Science gets most of its information by the process of reductionism, exploring the details, then the details of the details, until all the smallest bits of the structure, or the smallest parts of the mechanism, are laid out for counting and scrutiny. (p. 7)

The above definition of the scientific process created by Thomas (1974), may be paraphrased to define the abstracting process:

> Abstracts derive most of their substantive information by a process of reductionism, the analytical reading of the full text of a paper, monograph, or thesis, until all of the relevant parts of the structure and the essence of the findings and conclusions are laid out for writing and editing.

Primary authors should consider the process of writing abstracts to be an all-out effort in information reductionism or condensation, regardless of the style, content, or form that is required for the abstract. Reductionism also should be the primary consideration, no matter what type of written, spoken, or visual material is being abstracted, whether it be a monograph; a description of a scientific method; a statement of plans or policies; a review of the literature; an epidemiological survey; a mathematical analysis; an experimental study using materials, animals, or humans; a conference proceedings; a transcript of a hearing, or a personal-opinion paper based on practical experience or theoretical speculation.

Finally, authors should be unrelenting information reductionists throughout the full abstract preparation cycle of reading, thinking, writing, editing, or revising, whether these skills are used concurrently or sequentially. Throughout this preparation cycle, Strunk and White's (1979) terse advice to "omit needless words" to achieve conciseness therefore might be expanded as follows and applied unremittingly: Omit needless sentences and needless words and phrases within necessary sentences.

HANDLING MATERIALS

The following statement is from the instructions for the submission of abstracts for meetings convened by the Federation of American Societies for Experimental Biology (FASEB).

> 6.   **DO NOT ERASE**. Remember that your abstract will appear in *Federation Proceedings* exactly as you submit it; any erasures, smudges, errors, misspellings, poor hyphenations and deviations from good usage will be glaringly apparent in the published abstract.

The instructions are extremely detailed, because the large volume of these abstracts and rigid meeting deadlines necessitate that abstracts be submitted in "camera-ready copy." Consequently, they receive minimum editorial processing before they are printed in the journal *Federation Proceedings* and distributed at the FASEB meetings.

Even if abstracts that are submitted to other primary publishers will receive more prepublication editorial processing than the FASEB meeting abstracts, their authors should, nevertheless, prepare them with the same high degree of care as they would if the abstracts were, in fact, scheduled for treatment as camera-ready copy.

When the publisher furnishes instructions on abstract preparation, the author should read them carefully and prepare the abstract in strict compliance. In accordance with the design specifications for the full publication, the publisher determines the precise form in which the abstracts will appear. The readers of a particular publication become accustomed to the style in which abstracts are presented; therefore, unconventional forms should not be used. If, however, as an author you are convinced that the publisher's instructions hinder the writing of concise, informative or indicative abstracts, follow the instructions as completely as possible but, with your abstract, enclose separate, well-documented suggestions for improving the instructions.

A few general suggestions for preparing standard abstracts follow. The suggestions are based on practical experience, the FASEB instructions, and guidelines contained in the *American National Standard for Writing Abstracts* (ANSI, 1979).

1. Prepare an abstract that access information services can reproduce with little or no change, copyright permitting.

2. State the purpose, methods, results or findings, and conclusions or recommendations that are presented in the original document, either in that order or with initial emphasis on results and conclusions.

3. Make the abstract as informative as the nature of the document will permit, so that readers may decide, quickly and accurately, whether they need to read the entire document.

4. Unless otherwise instructed, use fewer than 250 words for most papers and portions of monographs and fewer than 100 words for notes and short communications. For long reports and theses, do not exceed 500 words.

5. Avoid including background information or citing the works of others in the abstract, unless the studies are replications or evaluations of their works.

6. Do not include information in the abstract that is not contained in the textual material being abstracted.

7. Verify that all quantitative or qualitative information used in the abstract agrees with the information contained in the full text of the document.

8. Use standard English and precise technical terms, and follow conventional grammar and punctuation rules.

9. Give expanded versions of lesser known abbreviations and acronyms, and verbalize symbols that may be unfamiliar to readers of the abstract.

10. Omit needless words, phrases, and sentences.

ADDING VALUE

> *Cost savings* to customers is an active decision by the service when it decides to use author abstracts rather than generate new ones. One can, of course, argue that there might be negative values resulting from the use of author abstracts. (Taylor, 1986, p. 112)

Taylor (1986), in his *Value-Added Processes in Information Systems,* a key source for this revised text (Chapter 10), does not identify any of the negative values to customers of abstracting and indexing services that might result if the services elect to use author abstracts. He also fails to list any other positive values that the use of such abstracts would add to the services other than the one of providing cost savings to customers.

No doubt Taylor would agree that other added values resulting from the use of properly written author abstracts within abstracting and indexing services could include

1. Higher technical quality, since the author is likely to be a subject expert.

2. Intrinsic value when the abstract integrates diverse elements of information into a tight unity.

MAKING MEANING

> Value is a matter of the unified coherence of a thing. The thing need not be linked with anything else, anything larger to have value. We need not look beyond something to find its (intrinsic) value, whereas we do have to look beyond a thing to discover its meaning. (Nozick, 1989, p. 167)

After striving to write a unified coherent abstract of an article or other piece of writing, the author need look no further than his or her work to assess the abstract's meaning (Chapter 11). Thus, by reviewing the text of the completed abstract against the full text of the material abstracted, more meaningful information may be discovered to add to it.

CHAPTER 3

Information Selection
and Relevance for Abstracts

*Programming the computer to select "significant represen-
tative sentences" required precise operational instructions,
and this in turn led to some understanding of how humans
select sentences, prepare abstracts, and evaluate the results.*
(p. 163)

—H. BORKO and C. L. BERNIER (1975)

IMPRESSIONISTIC ABSTRACTS

The results of "programming the computer to select 'significant representative sentences'" (Borko and Bernier, 1975) not only furnished insights into how humans select sentences from materials to be abstracted,
prepare abstracts, and evaluate the results, but also led to some understanding of how well the computer might, in turn, be programmed to select significant representative sentences and prepare abstracts. Borko
and Bernier concluded from their 1975 survey that computer systems
may select representative sentences, but they do not yet prepare abstracts—merely extracts. A review of the literature of the early 1990s
indicates that, essentially, this is still true. (See also Chapter 16 for
guidance in editing and revising computational abstracts.)

An evaluation of the content of abstracts in scientific and scholarly
publications and abstract journals, or those on file in data bases, also
would identify a few human-produced extracts that are mislabeled as ab-

stracts. The relative number of these extracts would serve as a good criterion for estimating the comparative value of the abstract journals or data bases. At their worst, computational and human-prepared extracts that are incorrectly labeled as abstracts are equivalent to a formless, impressionistic computer printout or typing of sentences on paper. At their best, these extracts serve as marginally acceptable substitutes for authentic abstracts.

Shortcomings in computational abstracts may be partially traced to the fact that techniques for preparing them have been in the development stage only over the second half of this century. In contrast, techniques for human preparation of abstracts have been developed and refined for at least three centuries.

Unlike the computer, humans have the proven potential to develop the reading, thinking, writing, editing, and revising skills that are prerequisites to the application of these techniques. When applied properly, the advanced techniques that are available to humans allow them not only to identify representative *sentences* but also to identify representative *information* in whatever form or location it appears in the materials to be abstracted and to format this information logically, reduce it coherently, and refine it concisely.

DIVERSITY AND COMPLEXITY OF MATERIALS TO BE ABSTRACTED

Drawing an analogy to the sport of golf may help to illustrate the diversity in form and the complexity in content of the materials that are abstracted. The type and total number of abstracts written by a prolific researcher over the course of a year or two or by a professional abstractor in a highly productive day's work might figuratively parallel the experience of a low-handicap golfer playing a round of golf on an 18-hole golf course. As with some of the golf holes, some of the 18 items to be abstracted will be lengthy and complicated, with a high potential for stymieing the abstractor. These will require using the highest skills, concentration, and energy to achieve good results.

Other items to be abstracted will be short and simple, permitting the author or the documental information processing abstractor to get straight to the point quickly, smoothly, and accurately using minimum strokes of the pen, typewriter, or word processor.

CONSTRUCTING WELL-CONSTRUED ABSTRACTS

> . . . the acts of mind involved in critical reading, in making sense of texts, are the same as those in operation when we compose: how we construe is how we construct. (Berthoff, 1978, p. 6)

The acts of mind involved in abstracting—in making concise sense of scientific, technical, and scholarly texts—also are based on well-construed elements of composition. The mental acts, as postulated here, are performed in four approximate stages: (1) focusing on the basic features of the materials to be abstracted; (2) identifying relevant information; (3) extracting, organizing, and reducing the relevant information into a coherent unit, usually one paragraph long; and (4) refining the completed abstract through editing and/or revising.

Focusing on Basic Features (Content Analysis)

The first step in the human abstracting process is to determine the general characteristics of the materials to be abstracted—the form, type, size, and structure of the information. The form may be a monograph, article, dissertation, project status report, or letter to the editor, to name a few. Different forms usually require slightly different abstracting procedures.

During the first stage, the materials to be abstracted must be clearly classified by the abstractor. Is the material based on experimental research or testing; epidemiological, etiological, sociological, or psychological surveys; descriptions of methods or equipment; theoretical research or mathematical modeling; or literature reviews, book reviews, or personal views on scientific, technical, or scholarly themes?

How is the text structured? Are primary and secondary headings used, particularly those containing such guide words as "introduction," "methods," "results," "conclusions," and "recommendations" that expedite locating representative information for the abstract? Are descriptions of original research readily identifiable, or will there be difficulty in separating them from background information during the succeeding stages of abstracting? For experimental research, are the methods and testing procedures conventional and simple to follow as described or are they unconventional and complicated?

Also, how much generalizing will be necessary to give a balanced, informative treatment in the abstract of the information on purpose, methods, results or findings, conclusions, and recommendations? If there are conclusions, are they presented unambiguously, are they scattered throughout the text, and will they be difficult to separate from the discussion of the work of other investigators?

Before beginning this first stage of abstracting, author abstractors are well aware of the information characteristics. Information processing service abstractors normally should be able to determine these characteristics in less than two minutes by scanning the materials to be abstracted.

Identifying Relevant Information

The second approximate stage in the abstracting process involves a rapid-review reading of the text to identify those portions that contain potentially relevant information for the abstract. (Some skilled abstractors complete this stage simultaneously while focusing on the basic features of the materials during the first stage.)

In a manner similar to the instructions formulated for some test programs for computer processing to select representative sentences from published materials, human abstractors seek relevant information for abstracts through identification of cue words or phrases in sentences in the text ("In this paper we," "Administration of," "Data were analyzed," "Results suggest"). As mentioned, abstractors also concentrate on the information presented under conventional functional headings such as "Introduction," "Methods," "Findings," and "Conclusions." The location of sentences within paragraphs is also a good indicator of potentially representative information for the abstract. The first or last sentences in a paragraph often, but not always, are topical or summary ones. Information that is identified through cue or function words and phrases or by locating topical sentences may then be used as a base for identifying additional, less-accessible, relevant information that has potential for extraction into the abstract.

Extracting, Organizing, and Condensing Relevant Information

After the most representative information for the abstract has been identified, the abstractor begins the "extracting into abstracting" stage. The extractable information is sorted mentally into a preestablished format. As mentioned, one standard format follows the sequence: purpose, methods, results, conclusions, and recommendations. Other formats generally involve rearrangement of these elements. (Relevant information frequently is not found for all of these elements; at times, spatial constraints may preclude use to only the most informative ones.)

Before writing, typing, or word processing the information for extraction into the abstract in the appropriate sequence, the abstractor reviews it for relevance and validity, then mentally condenses and consolidates it.

Information Refinement

The final stage in human abstracting involves editing or refining the raw abstract into a good informative or indicative abstract. The refinement process ranges from minor to major self-editing or revision by author or information processing abstractors, editors, or technical reviewers.

The following two examples of editing lengthy sentences to achieve conciseness were selected from a single abstract that had been reviewed by an editor for a documental information processing service.

Original Version:	*Edited Version:*
There were significant positive associations between the concentrations of the substance administered and mortality in rats and mice of both sexes.	Mortality in rats and mice of both sexes was dose related.
There was no convincing evidence to indicate that endrin ingestion induced any of the different types of tumors which were found in the treated animals.	For endrin ingestion, no treatment-related tumors were found in any of the animals.

SUMMARY OF HUMAN ABSTRACTING PROCESS

Figure 4 presents a recapitulation of the approximate stages followed by humans during the abstracting process. Figures 5 and 6 contain two examples of the results of the process.

Stages	Techniques	Results
1. Focusing on the basic features of the materials to be abstracted	Classifying the form and content of the materials	Determination of the type of abstract to be written, the relative length, and the degree of difficulty
2. Identifying the information (sometimes done simultaneously with Stage 1)	(a) Searching for cue or function words and phrases, structural headings and subheadings, and topic sentences; (b) expanding the search based on the results of (a)	Identification of a representative amount of relevant information for extraction
3. Extracting, organizing, and reducing the relevant information	Organizing and writing the extracted relevant information into an abstract, using a standard format	Preparation of a concise, unified, but unedited abstract (see Figure 5)
4. Refining the relevant information	Editing or reviewing the abstract by the originator or editorial or technical reviewers	Completion of a good informative or indicative abstract (see Figure 6)

Figure 4   Approximate stages in the human abstracting process.

Every cognitive skill draws upon part of the brain's extensive repertoire of representational subsystems, storage mechanisms, and processes. This tutorial article is an introduction to research exploring these basic components of cognitive skill and their organization. Four areas of research are reviewed: the perception of objects and words; the distinction between short- and long-term memory mechanisms; the retrieval of remembered episodes and facts; and attention, performance, and consciousness.

Figure 5   Stage 3 abstract. SOURCE: Monsell (1981, p. 378).

Research on the cognitive representational subsystems, storage mechanisms, and processes of the brain is reviewed tutorially. Studies of (l) the perception of objects and words; (2) short- and long-term memory; (3) the retrieval of remembered episodes and facts; and (4) attention, performance, and consciousness are described.

Figure 6   Stage 4 (edited) version of the Stage 3 abstract. SOURCE: **Adapted from the abstract in Monsell (1981) (Figure 5).**

CHAPTER 4

Analytical Reading

According to accepted theories, analysis (reduction to con-stituents) is the opposite of invention, which begins with con-stituents (material or abstract) and builds systems out of them. Now we are faced with the possibility that no such hard-and-fast distinction applies, and that in fact analysis is closely tied to invention. (p. 40)

—ROBERT GRUDIN (1990)

Good reading skills and habits are commonly accepted as prerequisites for effective writing in any form. Throughout the full abstracting process, the ability to read analytically is vital.

Preferably, analytical reading is done with rules and conventions for abstracting in mind, such as those given in the *American National Standard for Writing Abstracts* (ANSI, 1979), as supplemented by those special instructions on abstracting that have been developed by specific primary publishers or managers of information services and systems. Although the most proficient writers of abstracts can perform the reading and writing functions almost simultaneously, these functions will be discussed separately in this book for clarity of instruction.

QUALITY OF ABSTRACTS

As a simplified way of predicting the quality of abstracts, only through the development, application, and refinement of good analytical reading skills can good, better, or best abstracts be written, whether by authors or professional abstractors. The use of good reading skills, combined with average writing, editing, and revising skills, should result in the preparation of good-quality abstracts; the use of good reading and good writing skills, combined with average editing and revising skills, should result in the preparation of better quality abstracts; and the combined use of good reading, writing, editing, and revising skills should result in the preparation of the best-quality abstracts. According to this simple model, failure to develop, apply, and maintain all four of these communication skills will often result in the preparation of inferior abstracts.

ANALYTICAL READING SKILLS FOR ABSTRACTING

Analytical reading for abstracting involves reading actively for information content and passively for understanding during each of three reading stages. (Conversely, reading actively for understanding and passively for information content is more appropriate for research and writing activities that are more complex than abstracting.)

In the first or *exploratory-to-retrieval reading* stage, the abstractor rapidly reads through the full text to locate those sections that contain relevant information on the purpose, scope, methods, results or findings, and conclusions and recommendations.

In the second or *responsive-to-inventive reading* stage, the abstractor rereads the material that was identified during the first stage to select, extract, organize, synthesize, and write the most relevant information for the abstract.

During the final or *connective (value-to-meaning) reading* stage, the abstractor reads the abstract analytically to edit it for intrinsic unity and conciseness and then comparatively rereads it against the material from which it was written to ensure that tight external connections have been made to achieve maximum meaning. Adherence to the pertinent stylistic rules and conventions for abstracting is also verified. (Examples of the application of these reading techniques will be presented in succeeding chapters.)

THREE R'S FOR VERY-BEST-QUALITY ABSTRACTS

As previously stated, the use of good reading, writing, editing, and revising skills, combined with adherence to standard and special rules and conventions for abstracting, should result in the preparation of best-quality abstracts. Very-best-quality abstracts are attainable when the efforts of individual abstractors to *read* analytically and to *follow rules* carefully are supported directly or indirectly by cooperative professional *relationships* with other abstractors; with editors, technical reviewers, managers, or readers; or with other users of the abstracts, such as information processing indexers or information retrieval analysts. Parts II through V of this book emphasize the importance of "reading" and "rules"; Part VI emphasizes the importance of cooperative professional "relationships."

Candidate or practicing information processing abstractors who lack confidence in their analytical reading skills should attempt to obtain formal or informal training in advanced reading techniques. These techniques might include, but should by no means be limited to, speed reading. For self-instruction in analytical reading, the classic guidebook *How to Read a Book* (Adler and Van Doren, 1972) is highly recommended.

THE ADLER–VAN DOREN READING METHOD

> You are told about the various levels of reading and how to achieve them—from elementary reading through systematic skimming and inspectional reading, to speed reading. You learn how to pigeonhole a book, X ray it, extract the author's message, criticize. You are taught the different reading techniques for reading practical books, imaginative literature, plays, poetry, history, science and mathematics, philosophy and social science.

Adler's guidebook on reading was originally published in 1940 and went through many printings before he and Van Doren revised and updated it in 1972. The above paragraph was extracted from the text on the back cover of the revised paperback edition and serves well as a short descriptive abstract for the book. Chapters 4 through 9 of the book implicitly contain particularly relevant information, advice, and rules on reading in preparation for writing abstracts and on other conventional forms of documental information processing, such as indexing, cataloging, and translating. The later chapters contain guidance for reading that is associated with more complex research assignments such as reviewing, interpreting, and evaluating.

The rules in the early chapters of *How to Read a Book* have been used as a guide in compiling the following set of general reading rules for abstractors. Specific rules for exploratory-to-retrieval, responsive-to-inventive, and value-to-meaning reading will be introduced in later chapters.

GENERAL READING RULES FOR ABSTRACTING

Rule l. Read actively to identify information for the abstract and passively for understanding.

Rule 2. Read with standard rules and conventions and special instructions for writing abstracts in mind; for example, those of specific journals or access abstracting and indexing services.

Rule 3. Read attentively and enthusiastically (with eager interest and zeal) through the full abstracting process of reading, writing, self-editing, and revising.

PART II

EXPLORATORY-TO-RETRIEVAL READING AND RULES

INDICATIVE ABSTRACT

Stage 1, or exploratory-to-retrieval reading for abstracting, is described, and rules for such reading are presented. These rules are applied to the abstracting of two sample articles.

CHAPTER 5

Exploratory-to-Retrieval Reading
—Sample Abstract A

An abstract should be as informative as is permitted by the type and style of the document; that is, it should present as much as possible of the quantitative or qualitative information contained in the document. (p. 7)

—*American National Standard
for Writing Abstracts* (ANSI, 1979)

In this chapter and Chapter 6, the rules for exploratory-to-retrieval reading are applied to two sample articles for different types and styles of abstracting. These articles then are used to illustrate the second—responsive-to-inventive—reading stage for writing abstracts (Part III) and the third—value-to-meaning—reading stage for self-editing and revising abstracts (Part IV).

The articles used to write sample abstracts A and B were selected primarily for their diversity of information content, short to moderate length, and potential for demonstrating different forms of abstracts, since they had been previously abstracted by a computer-programmed abstracting system (these "computational" abstracts will be shown and edited and revised in Part V of this book).

31

DIFFERENCES IN READING BY AUTHOR AND DOCUMENTAL INFORMATION PROCESSING ABSTRACTORS

The discussion of exploratory-to-retrieval reading for Sample Abstract A is directed primarily to information processing abstractors and secondarily to authors who furnish abstracts with some of their scientific, technical, or scholarly writing. Information processing abstractors differ from primary authors who write their own abstracts by the speed with which they abstract, their relative objectivity, and the diversity of the materials that they abstract.

Professional abstractors normally have to meet more stringent deadlines than those required of primary authors and, therefore, must read at a faster rate. These abstractors read the material from "the outside in," since they are completely unaware of its contents. Reading from "the inside out," the author is thoroughly familiar with the contents and may even subjectively apply the results of the reading for abstracting to further modify the materials in his or her text. The information processing abstractor must remain completely objective throughout the abstracting process (unless she or he is preparing a critical abstract—a type of abstract seldom published in recent years). The professional abstractor also routinely abstracts a diverse selection of materials, many of which normally are abstracted only for bibliographic publications and information retrieval systems. The article selected for writing Sample Abstract A is one such example.

EXPLORATORY-TO-RETRIEVAL READING RULES

There are two rules for this form of reading. They should be observed in conjunction with the general reading rules given in Chapter 4. Exploratory-to-retrieval reading ideally is done once, nonstop, with a minimum of regressions and fixations. In practice, it may be necessary to repeat portions of this reading process.

Rule 1. Scan exploratively the text of the material to be abstracted to identify passages containing information having potential for retrieval for inclusion in the abstract.

Rule 2.   While scanning, mentally or in the margin of the copy, note those parts of the material that contain information on purpose, methods, findings, or conclusions and recommendations. (Some information processing abstractors may have to make their marginal notes lightly, for later erasure, if the material is the only copy held by their abstracting and indexing system or if it is on loan.)

EXPLORATORY-TO-RETRIEVAL READING FOR SAMPLE ABSTRACT A

The results of applying the two rules for this form of reading to the text of Sample Article A follow. Sample Article B, which is an article on experimental research, is discussed in Chapter 6.

The two reading rules, along with the general reading rules given in Chapter 4, have been applied to an article that was initially published in *Fortune* (Kain, 1969) without an abstract. The article is a critical review of a monograph on models for urban planning.

The vertical symbols in the left-hand margins denote paragraphs or tables containing background information (●); purpose, scope (or depth of coverage), and methods (▶); and conclusions and recommendations (☐). The actual writing of the abstract for this article is discussed in Chapter 8.

Sample Article A

---

① ● 　 The intense interest in the problems of
● the cities in recent years has produced a
● great outpouring of books diagnosing and
● proposing remedies for the "urban crisis."
The majority of these works are hardly no-
● ticed, being undistinguished and rather pal-
▶ lid imitations of one another. Jay W. For-
▶ rester's *Urban Dynamics* (M.I.T. Press)
▶ stands out in all this verbiage. The book
▶ has attracted attention because of the un-
▶ orthodoxy of Forrester's recommendations,
the self-assured manner in which he pre-
▶ sents them, and his prominent use of the
▶ prestigious tools of systems analysis. With
▶ so many insistent voices saying that cities
▶ need more financial help from state and fed-
▶ eral government, readers are likely to be im-
▶ pressed with Forrester's conclusion that help
from the outside may "worsen conditions"
▶ in cities. Forrester, moreover, makes it dif-
☐ ▶ ficult for readers to argue with him. With
☐ ▶ its appearance of rigor and scientism, its
☐ ▶ charts and diagrams, its arrays of numbers
printed out by a computer, *Urban Dynam-*
ics is rather intimidating.
② ▶ 　 Forrester, a professor at M.I.T.'s Sloan
▶ School of Management, relies on a comput-
▶ er model he developed to simulate the
growth, decline, and stagnation of a hypo-
▶ thetical city (or "urban area") from birth
☐ ▶ to old age (250 years). Such methods have
☐ ● a great deal of potential for the analysis of
☐ ● urban problems and have already demon-
☐ ● strated their value in a number of specific,
though limited applications. However, the
☐ ● development of truly useful and trustwor-

SOURCE: J. F. Kain. "A Computer Version of How a City Works." *Fortune,* November 1969, pages 241–242. Copyright © 1969 Time, Inc. All rights reserved. Reprinted by permission of *Fortune.*

Sample Article A (Continued)

☐ ● thy urban simulation models remains a dis-
☐ ● tant objective and will require much great-
☐ er resources than have yet been devoted to
☐ the task. Before adequate models become
available, many inadequate ones will be put
forward. Forrester's model is a conspicuous
☐ example. In his first chapter Forrester
▶ warns the reader that caution should be ex-
▶ ercised in applying the model to actual sit-
▶ uations. Subsequently, however, he ex-
▶ presses few reservations about the model's
▶ validity and freely uses it as a basis for pre-
▶ scribing public policy.

▶ ## A goal of minimum taxes

(3) ▶   The hypothetical city in *Urban Dynam-*
▶ *ics* is, in Forrester's words, "a system of in-
▶ teracting industries, housing, and people."
▶ At the start of the simulations there is only
▶ new industry in the city, but as time pass-
▶ es enterprises mature and then decline. The
▶ speed of this aging process depends on con-
▶ ditions in the city. As businesses pass
▶ through these successive stages, they em-
▶ ploy fewer workers and a smaller propor-
▶ tion of skilled workers.

(4) ▶   There are similarly three kinds of people
▶ in the city: "managerial-professional," "la-
▶ bor" (skilled or high-income workers), and
▶ "underemployed" (including unemployed
▶ and unskilled workers). And there are three
▶ kinds of housing, corresponding to the three
▶ kinds of people: premium housing, worker
▶ housing, and underemployed housing.

(5) ▶   The criteria used in evaluating the per-
▶ formance of the hypothetical city and the
▶ efficacy of alternative public policies are
▶ never explicitly set forth. However, min-
▶ imization of taxes per capita would be a
▶ fair rendering of the underlying criteria.
▶ Forrester seems to think that the objective
▶ of the city is to produce the lowest possi-
▶ ble tax rate.

(6) ▶   The fiscal relationships in Forrester's ur-
▶ ban system are intricate, but can be reduced
▶ to three fairly simple propositions: (1) Low-

Sample Article A (Continued)

▶ income households cost the city more in
▶ taxes than they pay, whereas the city makes
▶ a profit on high-income households. (2)
▶ Growing business enterprises are an un-
▶ qualified good because they pay taxes and,
▶ by assumption, cost the city nothing in ser-
▶ vices. (3) Increases in local taxes and in-
▶ creases in local government expenditures
▶ produce "adverse" changes in the city's
▶ population and employment structure. It
▶ follows from these propositions that "ur-
▶ ban-management policies" should be de-
▶ signed to encourage new enterprises and
▶ managerial-professional people to locate in
▶ the city and discourage low-skilled people
▶ from living there.

(7) ▶ The influence of tax rates on employment
▶ and population structure in Forrester's city
▶ is powerful and pervasive. "Managerial-
▶ professional" and "labor" families are as-
▶ sumed to be repelled by high tax rates,
▶ whereas the "underemployed" are indiffer-
▶ ent to them. High tax rates, moreover, dis-
▶ courage the formation of new enterprises
▶ and accelerate the aging of existing ones.
▶ There are still other adverse effects: high
▶ taxes retard construction of both premium
▶ and worker housing, which in turn discour-
▶ ages the kinds of people who live in these
▶ kinds of housing from moving to the city
▶ or remaining there.

(8) ▶ Increases in public expenditures, the oth-
▶ er half of the local fiscal equation, also have
▶ disastrous effects on the system. It is as-
▶ sumed that increases in expenditures per
▶ capita make the city no more attractive to
▶ high-income people and new enterprises,
▶ but make it substantially more attractive
▶ to low-income people. There are some small
▶ offsets in the positive effects of higher ex-
▶ penditures per capita on upward mobility
▶ from the underemployed class into the la-
▶ bor class; but these are overwhelmed by the
▶ direct and indirect effects on the size of the
▶ underemployed population.

(9) ▶ These examples are only a few of the "ad-

Sample Article A (Continued)

verse" consequences of higher taxes and increased public expenditures in Forrester's model. Since the model is so constructed that a development in one sector affects other sectors, these adverse effects cumulate throughout the system.

Help from an induced shortage

⑩ Forrester uses his simulation model to evaluate several "urban-management programs" that have been tried or proposed, and he concludes that they "may actually worsen the conditions they are intended to improve." For example, he finds that "financial support from the outside"—presumably including revenue sharing by the federal government—"may do nothing to improve fundamental conditions within the city and may even worsen conditions in the long run." But this conclusion is not at all surprising in view of what he does with the outside funds. Rather than using them to reduce or hold down city taxes, as proponents of such intergovernment transfers envision, Forrester uses them to increase city expenditures. Given the framework of his model, the net effects are inevitably adverse. If instead Forrester had used the outside support to reduce city taxes, the net effects would have been favorable to the hypothetical city. Virtually all of Forrester's evaluations of "conventional" policies are similarly flawed; none is a faithful rendering of policies it supposedly represents.

⑪ Considering the heavy emphasis Forrester puts on tax rates, it is striking that he fails to consider the costs of his principal recommendation: each year demolish 5 percent of the low-income housing. The costs of acquiring and demolishing the properties would increase city taxes, and, within the framework of the model, any increase in city taxes has adverse effects. But Forrester considers only the favorable effects of the demolition program. Given his model, these are considerable. The induced short-

Sample Article A (Continued)

▶ age of low-income housing makes the city
less attractive to low-income people; fewer
▶ come and more leave. (Where they go is a
question the model is not designed to consider.) As before, a decline in the ratio of
"underemployed" to total population
makes the city more attractive to high-income people, encourages formation of new
enterprises and construction of premium
and worker housing, and impedes deterioration of dwelling units and businesses. In
addition, the land cleared by increased demolition of low-income housing provides
space for new enterprises and for premium
and worker housing.

(12) The supply of vacant land is a critical
variable in Forrester's urban model. When
more than half the land is still vacant, using additional land produces increasingly
favorable effects. But once half the land in
the city has been put to use—which in the
simulations occurs at about 100 years—further depletions produce increasingly adverse effects. The city's growth is retarded, and stagnation and decline begin. As
more land is used up, the scarcity of vacant land slows formation of new enterprises and construction of premium and worker housing, and speeds obsolescence of both
enterprises and housing. Given the critical
role of land availability in the model, it
would appear that these adverse effects
could be staved off if the city could simply
extend its boundaries so as to absorb additional vacant land; but Forrester does not
deal with this possibility.

Where the solution lies

(13) Simplification is essential in computer
simulation models, and neither Forrester's
nor any other model can be criticized merely because it omits detail. But Forrester
omits some basic behavioral relationships.
The model's most serious weakness is that
the suburbs never explicitly appear in it.
For some simulation purposes, it might be

Sample Article A (Continued)

☐ permissible to disregard temporarily the in-
☐ terrelations between, say, the city and the
☐ rest of the nation beyond the metropolitan
☐ area. But what happens in a city strongly
☐ influences its suburbs, and vice versa. If the
☐ central city reduced its low-income popu-
☐ lation by 100,000, the low-income popula-
☐ tion of the suburbs would have to increase
☐ by roughly the same amount. Although
☐ Forrester's model reflects no awareness of
☐ this aspect of metropolitan interdepen-
☐ dence, suburban governments are all too
☐ aware of it. Indeed, much of the urban prob-
☐ lem today is a result of suburban govern-
☐ ments' successfully pursuing precisely the
☐ kind of beggar-thy-neighbor policies For-
☐ rester advocates for the central city.

⑭ ☐ Upon scrutiny, *Urban Dynamics* amounts
☐ to an intricate attempt to justify the re-
☐ sponses of big-city mayors to a harsh fiscal
☐ environment. Existing intergovernmental
☐ arrangements saddled them with awesome
☐ responsibilities for the nation's social prob-
☐ lems, but failed to provide them with com-
☐ mensurate financial resources. Much of the
☐ mayors' enthusiasm for now much-criti-
☐ cized urban-renewal programs is traceable
☐ to their desperate need for cash. In *Urban
☐ Dynamics*, pragmatic responses to an un-
☐ balanced allocation of responsibilities and
☐ tax resources are elevated to the status of
☐ rational and efficient policies for dealing
☐ with the complex web of problems popu-
☐ larly referred to as the "urban crisis."

⑮ ☐ The solution is not, as Forrester indi-
☐ cates, the pursuance of narrow self-inter-
☐ est by each local government. Instead we
☐ need to develop a more appropriate divi-
☐ sion of responsibilities and functions among
☐ governments, and thereby remove the fis-
☐ cal incentives for local governments to fol-
☐ low policies that, while perhaps efficient
☐ from the viewpoint of narrow self-interest,
☐ are inefficient from the viewpoint of soci-
☐ ety as a whole.   END

CHAPTER 6

Exploratory-to-Retrieval Reading
—Sample Abstract B

Readers for whom the document is of fringe interest often obtain enough information from the abstract to make their reading of the whole document unnecessary. Therefore, every primary document should include a good abstract. (p. 8)

—American National Standard for Writing Abstracts (ANSI, 1979)

Here, the two rules given in Chapter 5 for this form of reading, along with the general reading rules given in Chapter 4, have been applied to an article (Sample Article B) on experimental research that appeared in the *Journal of Physical Chemistry* (Klein and Scheer, 1970). The discussion of the abstracting process for this article is directed primarily toward authors of papers and monographs who must prepare their own abstracts and secondarily to information processing abstractors, particularly those who are in training to become abstractors.

Again, symbols have been inserted in the margin to designate passages in the article containing information of potential relevance to the abstract. These are for background information (●); purpose, scope (or depth of coverage), and methods (▶); results (□); and conclusions and recommendations (▷). The actual writing of the abstract for this article is discussed in Chapter 9.

Sample Article B

● **Introduction**

(1)   Reactions below about 150°K in the oxygen atom–olefin system occur without the formation of fragmentation products. A very decided advantage to studies in this temperature region is that the distinction between concurrent reaction paths characterized by small energy differences is emphasized. An example is provided in the comparison of the reactions of *cis*- and *trans*-2-butenes with O(^{3}P) at 90°K. *cis*-2-Butene gives approximately equal quantities of *cis*- and *trans*-2,3-epoxybutane. Of the epoxybutanes produced from *trans*-2-butene, 90% are *trans*.[1,2] It is well established that oxygen atom addition to olefins gives carbonyls as well as epoxides.[1,3] Carbonyl compounds can arise only by rearrangements in which either a hydrogen atom or an alkyl group is shifted from its original position on one of the olefinic carbon atoms. Both rearrangement processes, namely, the change of configuration in the epoxides from that of the parent olefin and the migration of a hydrogen atom or an alkyl group, are amenable to observation by previously developed, low-temperature methods. Several olefins were selected for study of the O atom addition to illuminate the nature of these rearrangements.

● **Straight-Chain, Internal Olefins**

(2)   The addition of O(^{3}P) to straight-chain, internal olefins is interesting because of *cis–trans* isomerism in the olefin and in the resulting epoxide compounds. A consideration of the O atom addition to *cis*- and *trans*-2-butene in the temperature region 77 to 113°K led to the formulation of a new transition intermediate.[2] In this intermediate, the oxygen atom is represented as bound in a loose, three-membered ring with, and in the plane of, the olefinic structure of the reactant. An interaction between the oxygen atom and the adjacent hydrogen atoms bonded to the olefinic carbon atoms is also postulated. The necessity for the as-

SOURCE: R. Klein and M. D. Scheer. "Addition of Oxygen Atoms to Olefins at Low Temperature. IV. Rearrangements." *Journal of Physical Chemistry*, 74(3):613–616, 1970. Copyright © 1970 American Chemical Society. Reprinted with permission.

Sample Article B (Continued)

sumption of this interaction arises from the observation that, for both *cis*- and *trans*-2-butene, the ratio of *cis*-2,3-epoxybutane to isobutyraldehyde, as well as that of *trans*-2,3-epoxybutane to 2-butanone, remains constant. The relationship holds over a wide temperature range (77–300°K), despite large differences in the ratios of *trans*- to *cis*-2,3-epoxybutane produced from *cis*- compared to *trans*-2-butene (1.25–8.3). Observations on 2-butenes have been extended to several more straight-chain, internal olefins in the low-temperature region. The results are given in Table I. Comparison of the *trans*-epoxide to ketone ratios from the *cis*- *vs.* the *trans*-olefin with increasing size of the olefin indicates that these ratios diverge. However, the larger olefins show greater stereospecificity in their reactions. Thus, *cis*-3-hexene gives about 2.5 times as much *cis*-3,4-epoxyhexane as the *trans*-epoxide. Even a relatively small quantity of 3-hexanone from the *cis* intermediate could easily account for the difference in the *trans*-epoxide/ketone ratio between the reactions of *cis*- and *trans*-3-hexene. It is noted that the recently proposed "epoxide-like" transition complex implies that, although only one form of the complex is possible from the *trans*-, two forms are possible from the *cis*-olefin

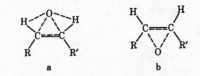

a   b

Of these, form b could readily lead to the ketone, because of easy migration of H, but form a would be expected to preponderate from the energetic viewpoint.

An indication of the importance of these forms, within the framework of the transition states specified and the assumption that form a gives only the aldehyde in its rearrangement to the carbonyl end product, whereas form b gives mostly ketones, is obtained from the data of Table I. The *trans*-olefin compounds, as may be noted, produce epoxides that contain 90–97% of the *trans* form. If the same ratio of *cis*-epoxide to aldehyde obtained from the *cis*-3-hexene is maintained in the *trans*-3-hexene products, the residual aldehyde presumed to arise from the *trans* intermediate may be calculated. Accordingly a ratio of 50:1 for the *trans*-epoxide/aldehyde compounds derived

Sample Article B (Continued)

Table I: Fractional Product Yields for the O(^{3}P) Addition to Internal, Straight-Chain Olefins at 90°K[a]

Products	2-Butene		2-Pentene		3-Hexene		4-Octene	
	cis	*trans*	*cis*	*trans*	*cis*	*trans*	*cis*	*trans*
trans-Epoxide	0.30	0.50	0.26	0.59	0.17	0.65	0.09	0.68
cis-Epoxide	0.24	0.06	0.34	0.04	0.42	0.02	0.82[c]	0.03[c]
Aldehyde	0.21	0.06	0.20	0.04	0.28	0.03		
Ketone	0.25	0.38	0.20[b]	0.33[b]	0.13	0.30	0.09	0.29
trans-Epoxide/ketone	1.2	1.3	1.3	1.8	1.3	2.2	1.0	2.3
cis-Epoxide/aldehyde	1.1	1.0	1.7	1.0	1.5	0.7		
cis-Epoxide/*trans*-epoxide	0.8	0.12	1.3	0.07	2.5	0.03		
Total epoxide/total carbonyl	1.2	1.3	1.5	1.7	1.4	2.0		

[a] The olefins were diluted 10:1 in propane prior to condensation on a 100-cm² Pyrex surface.   [b] Sum of 2-pentanone and 3-pentanone, not separated on the glpc.   [c] Sum of 2-propylpentanal and *cis*-4,5-epoxyoctane, not separated on the glpc.

Sample Article B (Continued)

from the *trans* complex is obtained. Clearly, aldehyde formation from the *trans* intermediate is negligible. All of the straight-chain olefins of Table I conform to this generalization. The *trans*-epoxide/ketone ratio obtained from the *cis*- as compared to the *trans*-olefin shows the largest difference with 4-octene. The correct value, 2.3, is obtained from *trans*-4-octene, because a contribution from the *cis* complex possible is virtually absent. This factor was used to calculate the ketone residual from the *cis* complex, starting with the *cis*-4-octene. Although the *cis*-epoxide and aldehyde were not separated, the ratio of the two may be assumed to be the same as the corresponding one from *cis*-3-hexene. The aldehyde/ketone ratio resulting from the *cis*-4-octene–oxygen complex is calculated to be about 7. It may be concluded that of the two forms of the transition complex derived from the *cis*-olefin, form a is the principal one and b is unimportant.

Two generalizations are apparent from Table I. The first is that retention of configuration of products becomes more pronounced with increasing chain length of the olefin. The second is that reaction of oxygen atoms in the low-temperature region tends to be more stereospecific with *trans*- than with *cis*-olefins. A stereotransformation of the transition intermediate requires a rotation of 180°, about the modified olefinic bond, of one of the carbon atoms of the double bond with its attached groups. Obviously, this process occurs with the *cis*-olefins. The extent to which stereotransformation will occur depends on the rates of ring closure and the rates of rearrangements leading to final products, compared to the rate of the *cis–trans* interchange in the complex. It seems reasonable to postulate that the rate of ring closure is independent of the size of the olefin. The ratio of total epoxide to total carbonyl products shows little change with size, and, hence, the rate of rearrangement to carbonyls is also size independent. The frequency of rotation of the portion of the complex

is then directly proportional to the extent of stereotransformation observed in the products. A measure of these transformations is the ratio of *cis*- to *trans*-epoxide, tabulated in Table I. In a rotationally unhindered system, the frequency is inversely related

Sample Article B (Continued)

to the moment of inertia of the rotating group. Qualitatively, it would be expected that because of the higher moment of inertia associated with the larger olefin, the stereospecificity should increase with size; this is indeed the case. It is interesting that *cis*-2-pentene shows more stereospecificity than *cis*-2-butene. Despite the fact that both compounds have a methyl group adjacent to the olefinic site, a larger rotational barrier is inferred to be associated with the 2-pentene. A quantitative consideration of the relationship of size and stereo effects would require that potential barriers for rotation be taken into account also, but the qualitative conclusions remain unaffected.

Group Migrations

Carbonyl compounds constitute a sizable fraction of the products of the oxygen atom addition to olefins in the low-temperature region and, as has been noted, an intramolecular group migration is required for carbonyl formation. The principal carbonyl product in the *trans*-2-butene reaction at 90°K is 2-butanone. The formation of this ketone requires the migration of H. Compared to migration .. the methyl group, that of H is highly favored. *cis*-2-Butene is not useful for the comparison, as both of the hydrogen atoms attached to the olefinic carbon pair are suppressed through interaction with oxygen in the complex. The relative quantities of 2-butanone to isobutyraldehyde, after correction of the latter for the contribution from the *cis* complex, is taken as a measure of the ratio of migration of the hydrogen atom to migration of the methyl group. At 90°K, it is about 30. Similar considerations for *trans*-3-hexene lead to a value of about 20 for the ratio of migration of hydrogen with respect to the ethyl group. If rates of migration are independent quantities, to be associated with the specific groups, the rate of migration of ethyl should be the same as, or slightly higher than, that of the methyl group. These ratios are imprecise, because of the small quantities of the aldehyde produced in each case. A direct comparison between methyl and ethyl migrations is desirable if their relative rates are to be established; this can be done through the use of 3,4-dimethyl-3-hexene (DMH). The O(^{3}P) reaction gives, in addition to 3,4-epoxy-3,4-dimethyl-hexane, two ketones, namely, 4,4-dimethyl-3-hexanone and 3-ethyl-3-methyl-2-pentanone, depending on whether the methyl or ethyl group migrates. The reaction gives no other products.

Sample Article B (Continued)

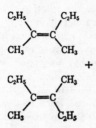

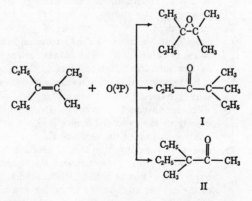

▶ Both *cis-* and *trans*-3,4-dimethyl-3-hexene were used.
▶ The two ketone products, 4,4-dimethyl-3-hexanone
▶ and 3-ethyl-3-methyl-2-pentanone, will be referred to
▶ as I and II. The use of 3-ethyl-2-methyl-2-pentene
▶ (MEP) furnishes further data for assessing the validity
▶ of the concept of relative rates of migration of groups
  in establishing the product ratios.

☐ The same two ketones are produced from MEP as
☐ from *cis-* and *trans*-DMH. The important difference

Sample Article B (Continued)

is that, whereas I results from the reactions of DMH with a rearrangement wherein a methyl group migrates, it is the migration of the ethyl group that gives I from MEP. Ketone II results from ethyl migration starting withD MH, or methyl migration starting with MEP. Therefore, if independent rates of migration are to be associated with these alkyl groups, the ketone ratio (I/II) produced from *cis-* or *trans-* DMH should be equal to (II/I) formed from MEP. It is emphasized that this follows if the presumed migration rates determine the position at which the O becomes localized. On the other hand, strong forces favoring addition to one of the olefinic carbons could control the alkyl group migrations.

Reactions were effected at 90°K in the apparatus routinely used for this purpose.[1] The olefins were diluted 10 to 1 with propane. The exposure time to oxygen atoms was 5 min, and about 1% of the olefin was reacted. The products were determined, after warmup, on a column (0.25 in. × 12 ft glpc) of Carbowax-6000, at 135° and a helium flow of 100 cc/min. The *cis* and *trans* isomers of 3,4-epoxy-3,4-dimethylhexane were not separable. Ketones I and II were easily separable. Retention times were determined with authentic samples of the two ketones. For all three olefins, only three glpc peaks were obtained for the products. These corresponded to the epoxides and the ketones I and II. Ratios of yield of product from the oxygen atom addition are given in Table II.

The notable feature of these results is that, of the two ketones, I and II, I is the major product; (I/II) = 2.5:1. Furthermore, this ratio is virtually independent of the starting olefin. Thus, the concept of independent rates of migration of groups in the rearrangement occurring in the O atom addition to olefins *must be abandoned*. The other alternative would require that the directive effect of the alkyl groups in MEP is such that the O adds to the carbon with the two ethyl groups 2.5 times more rapidly than to the carbon with the two methyl groups. It would appear that, insofar as the ratio of ketones is concerned, it is their relative stabilities that control the rearrangement processes. Transformation to final products is a migration of an alkyl group concerted with the localization of the oxygen atom on one of the carbon atoms. Localization of the oxygen atom in the transition complex *preceding* alkyl group rearrangement is not in accord with the experimental results. If, in fact, localization did occur,

Sample Article B (Continued)

▷ the migration would be determined, in part (completely,

Table II: Product Yield Ratios for the O(^{3}P) Addition to Some Isomeric Octenes at 90°K

Reactant	Ketone ratio (I/II)	Epoxides/ ketones
cis-DMH	2.5	1.9
trans-DMH	2.7	1.1
MEP	2.6	2.4

(Product ratios)

▷ if, as in MEP, the groups bonded to each of the olefinic
▷ carbon atoms occurred in pairs), by the directive factors,
▷ such as electron densities that are postulated as con-
▷ trolling the site of addition. It has been previously
● stated that oxygen atoms add mainly to the less-
● substituted carbon atom and that a methyl group con-
● fers "less substitution" than an ethyl group.[4] The
● directive influence of ethyl *vs.* methyl has been noted[5]
● for hydrogen atom addition to 2-pentene. At 90°K,
▷ the ratio of addition to C-2 is 1.6 times that to C-3.
▷ For MEP, addition of the O atom to that carbon atom
▷ of the double bond to which the two methyl groups are
▷ would, perforce, be formed in greater amounts than
▷ I; the data show unequivocally that this is incorrect.
⑧ ▷ The concerted rearrangement, in which oxygen
▷ localization and group migration occur, requires both
▷ electronic and spatial reorganization. The addition of
▷ ground-state, triplet oxygen to singlet-state olefin to
▷ give singlet-state products requires a relaxation process,
▷ as represented by a crossing of states on a potential
▷ surface. The recently introduced representation of
▷ the initial transition intermediate as a loose epoxide
▷ structure seems especially appropriate. Migration of
▷ groups probably involves a transient bridging of the
▷ double bond carbon pair. The path by which the
▷ intermediate relaxes to final products could even in-
▷ volve steric effects. The formation of the grouping

$$-C\begin{matrix} C_2H_5 \\ C_2H_5 \\ CH_3 \end{matrix}$$

▷ in II is sterically less favorable than

$$-C\begin{matrix} CH_3 \\ CH_3 \\ C_2H_5 \end{matrix}$$

Sample Article B (Continued)

▷ in I, and it may be speculated that the preponderance of
▷ I over II in the reactions of the *cis*- and *trans*-DMH and
▷ MEP can be ascribed to such steric effects.
▷   Table II shows an interesting variation among the
▷ three olefins as regards the epoxide/ketone ratio. The
▷ interpretation of these results, and, particularly, why
▷ MEP exhibits such a high epoxide/ketone ratio, is not
▷ yet at hand.

PART III

RESPONSIVE-TO-INVENTIVE
READING AND RULES

INDICATIVE ABSTRACT

Responsive-to-inventive reading, the second of the three reading stages for abstracting, is described. Rules for this form of reading are applied to the writing of two sample abstracts. The length and style of abstracts are discussed, as well as the time required to write them.

CHAPTER 7

Responsive-to-Inventive Reading for Abstracting

What is worth exploring is worth responding to. In a response, some action, emotion or judgment is contoured to the valuable panoply that is encountered, taking account of intricate features and fitting them in a nuanced and modulated way. A response differs from a reaction. A reaction focuses upon and takes account of a constricted, standard, preset group of features, and it issues as one of a limited number of preset actions. . . . In a full response, a large part of you responds to a large part of the situation by selection from a large range of nonstereotyped actions. (p. 44)

—ROBERT NOZICK (1989)

RESPONSIVE READING FOR WRITING ABSTRACTS

Responsive-to-inventive reading is the middle stage that begins the separation of man from machine or computer with regard to writing abstracts. Here cognitive skills are applied that are well beyond the capacity of present-day computer-programmed abstracting systems to emulate. In this stage, the extractable information that was identified in the exploratory-to-retrieval reading stage is responsively rather than reactively weighed for its potential to be transformed into the abstract.

Beginning author abstractors (of their own materials) obviously should not have any major problems in reading responsively for writing

53

an abstract, providing they follow the general rules for abstracting. For them, the pertinent information on purpose, scope, methodology, results or findings, and conclusions or recommendations should be conspicuously at hand.

Beginning abstractors for information processing systems likely will be less responsive and more reactive than authors when reading for the actual writing stage of abstracting. This may be evident in a tendency to be overresponsive to certain materials at the expense of overlooking more relevant materials elsewhere in the document being abstracted, thus leading to the writing of poorly balanced abstracts. They also may reactively extract a less-informative treatment of an important topic that appears early in a paper rather than read further to determine whether a more informative or succinct version of that topic exists.

Nevertheless, most novice information processing abstractors, who strive to become more responsive readers and are assisted in their efforts by instructors and editors, usually can become fairly proficient abstractors within two to three weeks, or a month at most. With further learning and practice, the results of their reading for abstracting should be more consonant with Nozick's (1989) thoughts on intellectual exploration: "Rather you explore in a place or direction you think is likely to be fruitful, and you allow things to roll in upon you, prepared to notice within general categories and to pursue interesting facts or possibilities further." (p. 44)

INVENTIVE READING FOR WRITING ABSTRACTS

> To some degree almost all human behavior is inventive, for it is seldom strictly repetitive and is aimed at contingencies which, though small and trivial, nevertheless require invention even of a humble kind. (Gregory, 1987, p. 389)

The transformation of extracted materials into a lucid abstract that resembles an Ashworthian "product of the highest craftsmanship" (Ashworth, 1973) often does require "invention of the humble kind" to answer many seemingly small and trivial questions.

A few examples of these questions are:

1. Is this paragraph or sentence that was selected for extraction definitely within the primary themes of the research or is it only peripheral to them?

2. How much space, if any, should I allow for the description of the methodology?

3. For this biomedical research paper, how many of the details on the therapeutic effects of the chemical compound should be extracted; how many on the side effects?

4. Do I need to verbalize any of the important symbols in this mathematical model?

5. Will the meaning of this acronym or eponym be self-evident to the likely readers of this abstract or must it be expanded or explained?

6. Will there be any significant loss in information content or readability if I consolidate these three sentences into one? Or have I already spent too much time on this abstract?

7. Have I extracted too much or too little information?

WRITING SKILLS FOR ABSTRACTING

Before closing this chapter with a listing of the suggested rules for responsive-to-inventive reading for the writing of abstracts, the writing skills necessary for abstracting will be discussed.

> But the main errors in his writing
> Are those common in his reading.
> (Tichy, 1966, p. vi)

Tichy (1966), in her guidebook *Effective Writing: For Engineers, Managers, and Scientists,* instructs "the professional man who is eager to write better" primarily in the fundamentals of writing and secondarily the fundamentals of reading so that he can "grasp the philosophy of style and apply the techniques with imagination and originality."

Most readers of this book will already have a sound grasp of the fundamentals of scientific, technical, and scholarly writing. If not, it is assumed that they are willing to supplement their knowledge on the broader principles of such writing, gained from reading this text, with more specialized training in writing skills through either formal or self-instruction courses.

For those with proven writing skills, the transition to writing abstracts should be a smooth, but not necessarily an effortless, one. Just as the athlete who is proficient in using the eye and hand skills necessary for playing competitive tennis has a head start if he decides to take up other racket sports, such as table tennis, squash, or racquetball, so does the individual with proven reading and writing skills in other writing forms have a head start in writing abstracts. His or her abstracts are not likely to be winning ones, however, until he or she learns and applies the methods and rules for this form of writing.

For those whose writing skills in scientific and scholarly literature are still in the early stages of development, the materials in this part of the book will be broadly beneficial. By themselves, however, they are not guaranteed to transform miraculously many, if any, novices into polished writers. For this to happen, more comprehensive, formal courses or self-instruction in writing techniques are advisable, combined with practical experience and the advice of proficient writers and good editors.

RESPONSIVE-TO-INVENTIVE READING RULES

There are up to four rules for this form of reading for writing abstracts. They are given below. In the next two chapters, the rules are used to write illustrative abstracts for the two sample articles that were introduced in Part II.

Rule 1. (*Step A*) Reread all of the information on purpose, scope, and methods (aboutness) that you identified during the exploratory-to-retrieval reading process. While reading, mentally index the primary and secondary themes that were described in this candidate material for the abstract, using your own choice of arbitrary terms or phrases. (Beginning abstractors or those writing an abstract for a complex document might find it helpful to jot down any arbitrary index terms or phrases on note paper.) (*Step B*) Write the primary aboutness part of the abstract (the first sentence).

Rule 2. If there is any other information on aboutness that you think is relevant to the abstract, write an additional sentence or sentences. If your instructions call for an indicative abstract, you have now completed the responsive-to-inventive reading stage and are ready to begin the value-to-meaning reading stage for self-editing of the completed abstract. If, however, you are writing an informative abstract, continue on to Rules 3 and 4, or to Rule 4 only, if you are writing an indicative–informative abstract.

Rule 3. (*Step A*) If you are writing an abstract for a document reporting on experimental research, tests, surveys, clinical case reports, or similar studies, reread the textual materials on the results or findings. While reading, condense this information mentally or write it on note paper, to aid your judgment of its relevance and significance. (*Step B*) Inventively extract the most relevant results and write them in sentence form, concisely, in descending order of significance.

Rule 4. (*Step A*) If the abstract does not already exceed word limitations, reread the conclusions and recommendations, if any, that were identified during the exploratory-to-retrieval reading process, as described in Rule 3. (*Step B*) Extract the most relevant conclusions and recommendations and write them in sentence form, tersely, in descending order of significance, to the full extent that space for the abstract remains.

CHAPTER 8

Responsive-to-Inventive Reading
—Sample Abstract A

*I always have two things in my head—I always have a theme
and the form. The form looks for the theme, the theme looks
for the form, and when they come together you're able to
write.* (p. 328)

W. H. AUDEN (In: Osborne, 1979)

During the exploratory-to-retrieval reading process discussed in Chapter
5, the purpose, scope, methods, and conclusions "themes" for writing the
abstract for Sample Article A were identified. Applying rules 1 and 2 of
responsive-to-inventive reading, an indicative abstract for this paper will
now be prepared; then the abstract will be transformed into an indicative–informative one by applying Rule 4, to add "conclusion-like" information. (Rule 3 on the writing of information on results does not apply
to Sample Article A, since it is a book review not an experimental study,
survey, or investigation.) But first, a brief discussion of some matters
relating to the "themes and forms" of abstracts.

LENGTH OF ABSTRACTS

Although some primary publishers or contractors for bibliographic information services specify the exact length that the abstracts should be
("150 words," "200 words," etc.), most specifications for the length of

abstracts are properly less specific ("approximately 150 words," "in 200 words or less"). The more general instructions are more appropriate because the length is mainly a function of the type and content of the information contained in the material being abstracted. The *American National Standard for Writing Abstracts* (ANSI, 1979) uses the qualifier "fewer" when recommending the number of words to be used:

> For most papers and portions of monographs, an abstract of fewer than 250 words will be adequate. For notes and short communications, fewer than 200 words should suffice. (p. 9)

Mary-Claire van Leunen (1978), in *A Handbook for Scholars,* measures the length of abstracts in minutes of reading time: "In fact, a good device for writing abstracts is to pretend that you're in a phone booth, making a long-distance call to a colleague. You want to give him the gist of your latest paper, and you have change for only three minutes." (p. 106) The three minutes should be more than adequate for reading the content of most abstracts. For many abstracts, the author should have enough time left over in the phone call after reading the abstract to mention the status of his or her current research and future plans.

STYLE OF ABSTRACTS

> That style is best in an abstract which more *quickly* conveys the necessary information. Clarity is essential; vividness is not. . . . Brevity is important but is to be measured by the amount of information conveyed in a given space, not by the number of lines. (p. 153)

Borko and Chatman (1963), in their survey of abstractors' instructions, quoted the above instructions on style from the policies and procedures for *Psychological Abstracts.* The survey was done to develop a set of criteria for judging the adequacy of an abstract.

Concern for the structure, style, and content of abstracts is important during both the writing and self-editing phases of abstracting. But further discussion of these matters will be deferred (see Chapter 9) until provisional versions of the two sample abstracts have been written and discussed in this and the next chapter.

RESPONSIVE-TO-INVENTIVE READING OF SAMPLE ARTICLE A, RULE 1

With the general rules and conventions for writing an informative abstract in mind, the abstract for Sample Article A will now be written. Step A of Rule 1 for responsive-to-inventive reading states: *Reread all of the information on purpose, scope, and methods (aboutness) that you identified during the exploratory-to-retrieval reading process. While reading, mentally index the primary and secondary themes that were described in this candidate material for the abstract, using your own choice of arbitrary terms or phrases. (Beginning abstractors or those writing an abstract for a complex document might find it helpful to jot down any arbitrary index terms or phrases on note paper.)*

Sample Article A is a review of a book. Twelve of the paragraphs in the article contain information on the purpose and scope of the book. In the extracts of two of these paragraphs (below), arbitrary index terms have been inserted in brackets at the end of each paragraph. This is a convenient way to illustrate this procedure, but it is too formalized and time-consuming to be recommended for general practice. Mental indexing or jotting down the arbitrary terms or phrases informally is preferable. Sample versions of the responsive-to-inventive reading and arbitrary indexing for the other 10 paragraphs in Sample Article A, containing information on purpose and scope, are presented in Appendix 6.

[Paragraph 1] Jay W. Forrester's *Urban Dynamics* (M.I.T. Press) stands out in all this verbiage. The book has attracted attention because of the unorthodoxy of Forrester's recommendations, the self-assured manner in which he presents them, and his prominent use of the prestigious tools of systems analysis. With so many insistent voices saying that cities need more financial help from state and federal government, readers are likely to be impressed with Forrester's conclusion that help from the outside may "worsen conditions" in cities. Forrester, moreover, makes it difficult for readers to argue with him. With its appearance of rigor and scientism, its charts and diagrams, its arrays of numbers printed out by a computer, *Urban Dynamics* is rather intimidating. [INDEX TERMS: book review; systems analysis; urban dynamics]

[Paragraph 12] The supply of vacant land is a critical variable in Forrester's urban model. When more than half the land is still vacant, using additional land produces increasingly favorable effects.

But once half the land in the city has been put to use—which in the simulations occurs at about 100 years—further depletions produce increasingly adverse effects. The city's growth is retarded, and stagnation and decline begin. As more land is used up, the scarcity of vacant land slows formation of new enterprises and construction of premium and worker housing, and speeds obsolescence of both enterprises and housing. [INDEX TERMS: land use; urban growth/decline; housing; industry]

Once the abstractor has rapidly reread and created a mental or written index of the article's aboutness information, the primary aboutness sentence can be written, in accordance with Step B of Rule 1. The writing process involves conventional, logical, and grammatical techniques. The mechanics of these techniques are discussed in detail in other parts of this text or are inferred in the makeup of the sentences prepared for sample abstracts A and B in this chapter and Chapter 7, as well as in other examples of abstracts included in this text, particularly those in Chapters 14–16.

A suggested version of the primary aboutness sentence for Sample Abstract A follows.

The use of systems-analysis techniques and computer modeling as described by Jay W. Forrester in his book *Urban Dynamics* is evaluated.

Rule 2 may now be applied to complete the aboutness information in the abstract. The following two sentences describe the scope of the remaining purpose information.

The interrelationships of public policy and financing, taxes, municipal expenditures, employment, housing, and population mobility are discussed. The effects of land supply and use also are considered.

SAMPLE ARTICLE A—CONCLUSIONS/ RECOMMENDATIONS

If an indicative abstract was all that was required for this article, the responsive-to-inventive reading for writing the abstract now would be completed. The next step would be to begin the value-to-meaning read-

responsive-to-inventive reading process further, however, the abstract can be transformed into an indicative–informative one by applying Rule 4, to add "conclusion-like" statements. Such statements may take the form of straightforward conclusions or be associated with opinions, judgments, recommendations, suggestions, implications, evaluations, applications, new relationships, or hypotheses accepted or rejected.

Seven of the 14 paragraphs in the article contain information on the conclusions and recommendations of the book reviewer. The results of responsive reading for one of these paragraphs are shown below. The results of responsive reading for the other six paragraphs are illustrated in Appendix 6.

> [Paragraph 1] . . . With its appearance of rigor and scientism, its charts and diagrams, its arrays of numbers printed out by a computer, *Urban Dynamics* is rather intimidating. [INDEX TERMS: intimidating use of charts, diagrams, and computer data]

After rapidly rereading all of the paragraphs containing information on conclusions and recommendations, the informative portion of the abstract may be written in accordance with Step B of Rule 4. A suggested version follows.

> The reviewer concludes that many of the urban management policies proposed in *Urban Dynamics* are inadequate or unrealistic. The significance of taxes and pragmatic financing of urban-renewal programs is overemphasized, and the cost of demolishing low-income housing and the potential for using vacant lands beyond city limits are overlooked. Responsibilities and functions of local governments should be redistributed to avoid pursuance of narrow self-interests. The reviewer recommends that funding from nonlocal sources should be used to reduce municipal taxes rather than to increase municipal expenditures.

The provisional writing of a full indicative–informative abstract for Sample Article A is now complete. Self-editing of the abstract through value-to-meaning reading is described in Chapter 12.

CHAPTER 9

Responsive-to-Inventive Reading —Sample Abstract B

There are twenty crucial minutes in the evolution of my paintings. The closer I get to that time—those twenty minutes—the more intensively subjective I become—but the more objective, too. Your eyes get sharper; you become continuously more critical. (p. 42)

—PHILIP GUSTON (1980)

TIME REQUIRED TO WRITE ABSTRACTS

Little is written in the recent literature on how long it takes an information processing abstractor to write an abstract. This is probably a consequence of the difficulties involved in measuring or estimating the time that is needed.

One measurement problem stems from the fact that information processing abstractors—working at information system facilities or freelance—may write original abstracts on simple or complex themes, edit or modify author abstracts, or write translation abstracts. Each task has its own range of time requirements.

Usually, the information in the materials to be abstracted is presented concisely and in a unified manner, and the information on purpose, scope, methods, results or findings, and conclusions or recommendations can be located with little difficulty. Occasionally, however, the information is written incoherently or ambiguously, or is poorly organized, and extra time and effort are required during the retrieval- and inventive-reading processes for abstracting.

Nevertheless, the 20-minute spell of creativity that was discussed by the late American artist Philip Guston (1980) serves well as an approximate figure for gauging the time that it should take a highly proficient information processing abstractor to write an original abstract of a difficult paper. Novice abstractors could take twice that time or longer.

By original abstracts, I mean those for which the abstractor is instructed to concentrate on the materials in the body of the document while ignoring completely the author's abstract, if one is present, and preferably the author's title as well. The same proficient abstractor might take only 12 minutes to write an abstract for a short uncomplicated paper or monograph. The 12 to 20 minutes would be spent roughly as follows::

exploratory-to-retrieval reading	3 to 5 minutes
responsive-to-inventive reading	8 to 12 minutes
value-to-meaning reading	1 to 3 minutes

After spending 12 to 20 minutes writing an abstract, the information processing abstractor should take a short mental break of three to five minutes. The exact length of the break will depend on whether the abstractor next will write another original abstract or will do the less-difficult task of modifying or editing an author's abstract.

Abstracting services that require the abstractor to catalog bibliographic data or record index terms should allow an additional 5 to 10 minutes of processing time for each abstract.

RESPONSIVE-TO-INVENTIVE READING OF SAMPLE ARTICLE B—RULE 1

The rules for responsive-to-inventive reading will now be applied to the writing of indicative and informative versions of Sample Abstract B. Step A of Rule 1 for this reading states: *Reread all of the information on purpose, scope, and methods (aboutness) that you identified during the exploratory-to-retrieval reading process. While reading, mentally index the primary and secondary themes that were described in this candidate material for the abstract, using your own choice of arbitrary terms or phrases. (Beginning abstractors or those writing an abstract for a complex document might find it helpful to jot down any arbitrary index terms or phrases on note paper.)*

During the retrieval reading of Sample Article B, information on purpose, scope, and methods was located, either explicitly or implicitly, in five of the nine paragraphs (1–3, 5, and 6) and one of the two tables (Table 1) in the paper. Extracts of two of these paragraphs are shown below with arbitrary index terms.

[Paragraph 1] Both rearrangement processes, namely, the change of configuration in the epoxides from that of the parent olefin and the migration of a hydrogen atom or an alkyl group, are amenable to observation by previously developed, low-temperature methods. Several olefins were selected for study of the O atom addition to illuminate the nature of these rearrangements. [INDEX TERMS: rearrangements; epoxide configuration; hydrogen atom or alkyl group migration; low temperature]

[Paragraph 2] The addition of $O(^3P)$ to straight-chain, internal olefins is interesting because of *cis-trans* isomerism in the olefin and in the resulting epoxide compounds. A consideration of the O atom addition to *cis-* and *trans*-2-butene in the temperature region 77 to 113°K led to the formulation of a new transition intermediate. In this intermediate, the oxygen atom is represented as bound in a loose, three-membered ring with, and in the plane of, the olefinic structure of the reactant. An interaction between the oxygen atom and the adjacent hydrogen atoms bonded to the olefinic carbon atoms is also postulated. . . . Observations on 2-butenes have been extended to several more straight-chain, internal olefins in the low-temperature region. [INDEX TERMS: *cis-trans* isomerism; epoxides; 2-butene; straight-chain, internal olefins; low temperature; transition intermediate]

The extracts of these two paragraphs on the purpose, scope, and methods in Sample Article B should adequately demonstrate the first step in Rule 1 of the responsive-to-inventive reading process. This analytical reading permits information processing abstractors to grasp the information content of the paragraphs more thoroughly and aids author abstractors in identifying clearly those details in their work that are relevant for consideration during the writing of the first sentence of the abstract (Rule 1, Step B). No further extracts from the article for this part of the abstract will be given here. A more complete version of the results of the responsive-to-inventive reading and arbitrary-indexing process for Sample Abstract B is provided in Appendix 7.

RESPONSIVE-TO-INVENTIVE READING—RULE 1, STEP B

The second step in Rule 1 for responsive-to-inventive reading covers the writing of the primary aboutness sentence of the abstract, based on the results of rereading and weighing the relative significance of candidate information on the purpose, scope, and methods in the sample article.

As often happens, the introductory material in paragraph 2 of the article contains the most significant leads for completing this step. This material, supplemented by other information on purpose, scope, and methods in the other four paragraphs and in Table 1, was used to write the following primary aboutness sentence.

> The effects of oxygen atom addition to olefins on epoxide configuration rearrangements and migration of hydrogen and methyl and ethyl groups were studied at 90°K by using gas-liquid chromatography.

SECONDARY ABOUTNESS SENTENCE(S)—RULE 2

If there is any other information on aboutness that you think is relevant to the abstract, write an additional sentence or sentences.

As already mentioned, for many short abstracts, or for longer ones in which the information on purpose, scope, and methods is covered adequately in the first sentence, this rule does not apply. Two secondary aboutness sentences, however, are proposed for Sample Abstract B:

> *Cis-trans* isomerism in straight-chain, internal olefins and resulting epoxide compounds was determined. *Cis-* and *trans*-epoxide, aldehyde, and ketone product-yields were calculated, as well as ketone and epoxide product-yield ratios for the addition of O(^{3}P) to *cis-* and *trans*-2-butene, 2-pentene, 3-hexane, and 4-octene and *cis-* and *trans*-3,4-dimethyl-3-hexene (DMH) and 3-ethyl-2-methyl-2-pentene (MEP), respectively.

RESULTS INFORMATION—RULE 3

(Step A) If you are writing an abstract for a document reporting on experimental research, tests, surveys, clinical case reports, or similar studies, reread the textual materials on the results or findings. While reading, condense this information mentally or write it on note paper, to aid your judgment of its relevance and significance.

Results information in Sample Article B was discussed by the authors in paragraphs 2, 3, 5, and 6. An approximate version of the results of applying Step A of Rule 3 to two of these four paragraphs follows:

> [Paragraph 3] The *trans*-olefin compounds, as may be noted, produce epoxides that contain 90–97% of the *trans* form. . . . Accordingly a ratio of 50:1 for the *trans*-epoxide/aldehyde compounds derived from the *trans* complex is obtained. . . . The *trans*-epoxide/ketone ratio obtained from the *cis*- as compared to the *trans*-olefin shows the largest difference with 4-octene. . . . The aldehyde/ketone ratio resulting from the *cis*-4-octene-oxygen complex is calculated to be about 7. [INDEX TERMS: *trans*-olefins produced *trans*-epoxides; differences in *trans*-epoxide/aldehyde ratios and *trans*-epoxide/ketone ratios]

> [Paragraph 5] The $O(^3P)$ reaction gives, in addition to 3,4-epoxy-3,4-dimethylhexane, two ketones, namely, 4,4-dimethyl-3-hexanone and 3-ethyl-3-methyl-2-pentanone, depending on whether the methyl or ethyl group migrates. The reaction gives no other products. . . . The same two ketones are produced from MEP as from *cis*- and *trans*-DMH. . . . Ketone II results from ethyl migration starting with DMH, or methyl migration starting with MEP. [INDEX TERMS: oxygen addition to DMH produces 3,4-epoxy-3,4-dimethylhexane and two ketones; ketone II results from ethyl or methyl migration]

Step B of rule 3 specifies: *Inventively extract the most relevant results and write them in sentence form, concisely, in descending order of significance.* The results information reported in the abstract also should be consistent with the information on purpose, scope, and methods given in the first part of the abstract. Suggested results sentences for Sample Abstract B are:

Comparison of the *trans*-epoxide to ketone ratios from the *cis-* vs. the *trans*-olefin indicates that these ratios diverged with increasing size of the olefin. Reactions of larger olefins were more stereospecific; *cis*-3-hexene gave about 2.5 times as much *cis*-3,4-epoxyhexane as the *trans*-epoxide. *Trans*-olefin compounds produced epoxides containing 90–97% of the *trans* form, resulting in a 50:1 ratio for the *trans*-epoxide/aldehyde compounds from the *trans* complex. The *trans*-epoxide/ketone ratio obtained from the *cis-* as compared to the *trans*-olefin showed the largest difference with 4-octene. Besides 3,4-epoxy-3,4-dimethylhexane, oxygen addition using DMH gave 4,4-dimethyl-3-hexanone (I) and 3-ethyl-3-methyl-2-pentanone (II) ketones, depending on whether the methyl or ethyl group migrated. The reaction gave no other products. Using MEP the same two ketones were produced as from *cis-* and *trans*-DMH; but ketone (I) resulted from methyl and ethyl group migration, starting with DMH and MEP, respectively. Opposite migrations produced ketone II.

CONCLUSIONS INFORMATION—RULE 4

(Step A) If the abstract does not already exceed word limitations, reread the conclusions and recommendations, if any, that were identified during the exploratory-to-retrieval reading process, as described in Rule 3. (Step B) Extract the most relevant conclusions and recommendations and write them in sentence form, tersely, in descending order of significance, to the full extent that space for the abstract remains.

The final sentences in Sample Abstract B will contain conclusions information only. No recommendations were presented in the sample article. The authors did present a significant amount of discussion in seven paragraphs of the article on their conclusions based on the research findings. The following seven sentences were extracted and modified for the abstract from two of these paragraphs (4 and 8). Appendix 7 contains illustrations of the responsive-to-inventive reading process for all seven of the paragraphs.)

Results suggest that retention of configuration of products is dependent on olefin chain length, and that reaction of oxygen atoms at low temperature is more stereospecific with *trans*-olefins. Stereotransformation of the transition intermediate requires a 180° rotation of one of the carbon atoms of the double bond with its attached groups about the modified olefinic bond, which occurs with the *cis*-olefins. Stereotransformation is a factor of rates of ring closure and rearrangement leading to final products, compared to the *cis-trans* interchange in the complex. Ring closure probably is independent of olefin size. Concerted rearrangement involving oxygen localization and group migration requires electronic and spatial reorganization. Addition of ground-state, triplet oxygen to singlet-state olefin to give singlet-state products probably requires a relaxation process. Group migration probably involves a transient bridging of the bond carbon pair, and intermediate relaxation to final products could involve steric effects.

Provisional abstracting of Sample Article B is now complete. The abstract was purposefully made much lengthier than is normal for an article of the type and length of the sample one. This was done to demonstrate amply the kinds of information that have potential for inclusion in the abstract and, subsequently, to show how the size can be reduced by applying the rules for value-to-meaning reading for the self-editing of abstracts. The application of these rules is described in Chapter 13.

PART IV

CONNECTIVE (VALUE-TO-MEANING) READING AND RULES

INDICATIVE ABSTRACT

The significance of value and meaning within documental information processing is examined. Value-to-meaning reading techniques for the self-editing and revising of abstracts by authors and information processing abstractors are described. Rules for value-to-meaning reading are demonstrated in the editing of two sample abstracts.

CHAPTER 10

Connective (Value-to-Meaning) Reading: 1. Value

The abstractor should develop the practice of critically re-reading the completed abstract and should chop ruthlessly at all the verbiage before forwarding it to the reviewer. (p. 153)

—*Guide to Abstracting and Indexing for Nuclear Science Abstracts* (In: Borko and Chatman, 1963)

The second stage—responsive-to-inventive reading, which was discussed in Part III—is done to record rapidly in the required format (hand- or typewritten on paper or entered into a word processor) the most relevant information from the material being abstracted. Rules and conventions for abstracting are important during this process but are not the primary concern. They should not interfere with the smooth flow of writing.

Rules and conventions for coherent, concise, and idiomatic writing, however, become a primary concern during "Connective (Value-to-Meaning) Reading," the third and final stage of analytical reading for abstracting. In the first edition of this guidebook, the third reading stage was called "Critical Reading," which essentially it is. But here it is examined more broadly and deeply, based on the concepts of meaning and value. A goal of this final reading of the completed version of the draft abstract is to ensure that it contains adequate value and meaning, and, if not, to add more of these qualities to it.

To gain some perspective on the concept of value, the remainder of this chapter will be an overview of the philosophical, economic, and information processing values, respectively, of things, information systems, and information representations, including abstracts. Meaning will be discussed in the next chapter; then the concepts of adding value and making meaning while abstracting will be applied during the editing of sample abstracts A and B in Chapters 12 and 13.

THE PHILOSOPHICAL VALUE OF THINGS

Nozick's (1989) book of philosophical meditations, *The Examined Life,* has no back-of-the-book index. My own construction of a slanted index to his book, to the term "value" only, reveals that 84 of its 303 pages (27 percent) contain substantive information on this term. These pages can be further indexed to 20 subheadings for value, the 5 most salient of which are: value and reality (discussed on 15 pages), value and importance (on 9 pages), value and emotions (on 9 pages), intrinsic value (on 8 pages), and value and organic unity (on 8 pages). A portion of the textual content for the last two subheadings epitomizes what is relevant to this text in Nozick's definitions:

> *Intrinsic Value.* The notion of value is not simply some vague laudatory term. Some things have value only as a means to something else that is valuable. And some things have a value of their own, an intrinsic value. (Some things have both kinds of value, value as a means to something else and also a value of their own.) This notion of intrinsic value is the basic one; other kinds of value exist by their relation to intrinsic value.   (pp. 163–164)

> *Organic Unity.* The greater the diversity that gets unified, the greater the organic unity; and also the tighter the unity to which the diversity is brought, the greater the organic unity. . . . Something has intrinsic value, I suggest, to the degree that it is organically unified. Its organic unity *is* its value.   (p. 164)

The roles that intrinsic value and organic unity play in connective reading for abstracting will be examined at the close of this chapter.

THE ECONOMIC ADDED-VALUE OF INFORMATION SYSTEMS

In his ground-breaking book, *Value-Added Processes in Information Systems,* Taylor (1986) contends that the value-added spectrum for information systems generally proceeds in complexity from the organizational, analytical, and judgmental to the decision processes. Within this spectrum, value can be interpreted in four possible ways, which may be viewed in terms of:

1. The value added or added value as used in economics.

2. The characteristics or attributes that are added to the data and information items being processed that make them more useful to users, clients, or customers.

3. The exchange value, or an extension of this: apparent value.

4. The value associated with the client or user and the context within which information is used.

The primary concerns of information processing in this text are the initial segment of Taylor's value-added spectrum—organizing information—and his second interpretation of value in information systems; that is, the characteristics or attributes that are added to the data and information items being processed that make them more useful to users, clients, or customers.

For his value-added model of information systems, Taylor also identifies 23 values and elaborates on how they may be added to library and abstracting and indexing systems and services and in information analysis and decision-making contexts. Of these 23 values, Taylor states that at least 9 can be added during the abstracting process. These nine values are intellectual access III (that is, noise reduction, which is done to "reduce or compress large amounts of information into compact items"); accuracy; cost savings; formatting; interfacing I (that is, mediation, ease of use, or the "means used to assist users in getting answers from the system"); physical accessibility; precision; reliability; and response speed.

On page 246 of *Value-Added Processes in Information Systems,* Taylor lists 10 value-added activities in abstracting during which these values can be added:

Value-added Activities	*Values Added*
1. Use subject specialists as abstractors	Access III (subject summary, noise reduction)
2. Provide in-house training for abstractors	Accuracy, reliability
3. Use author abstracts	Cost savings
4. Send request to journal editors that abstracts printed in journals be improved	Reliability
5. Prepare informative abstracts	Interfacing I (mediation, ease of use)
6. Prepare indicative abstracts for conference proceedings	Access III (subject summary, noise reduction)
7. Slant abstracts to users	Precision
8. Use standardized format for abstracts	Reliability, formatting
9. Have two-week quality control cycle: editing, proofing	Accuracy, response speed
10. Have abstracts available online (in-house processing)	Physical accessibility, accuracy

VALUE-ADDED PROCESSING OF DOCUMENTAL INFORMATION

It would make an absorbing essay in the intellectual history of the last quarter-century to trace what happened to the originating impulse of the cognitive revolution, how it became fractionated and technicalized. . . . Very early on, for example, emphasis began shifting from "meaning" to "information," from the *construction* of meaning to the *processing* of information. The key factor in the shift was the introduction of computation as the ruling metaphor and of computability as a necessary criterion of a good theoretical model. . . . But [computational] information processing cannot deal with anything beyond well-defined and arbitrary entries that are strictly governed by a program of elementary operations. Such

a system cannot cope with vagueness, with polysemy, with metaphoric or connotative connections. (Bruner, 1990, pp. 4–5)

As the psychologist Bruner (1990) notes in his book, *Acts of Meaning,*
one new form of information processing is done computationally and
mainly by programming computers. Computational information processing differs radically from the older form of manual processing that is the
subject of this text: documental information processing. The latter is
done mentally as well as computationally by humans who, unlike the
computer, are capable of coping with vagueness, polysemy, and
metaphoric or connotative connections. In this form of processing, information in various types and forms of documents is organized into representations. After this processing is done by humans, many of these
documental information representations are entered into computers for
storage, manipulation, and retrieval. Some examples of representations
that are products of documental information processing are abstracts, indexes, translations, definitions, catalogs, bibliographies, glossaries,
dictionaries, encyclopedias, concordances, thesauri, and other reference
materials.

Below, for illustration, value-adding information processes that are
applied during the functions of indexing and translating documents are
examined before connective reading and the value-adding processing of
abstracts are considered.

Value-adding Indexing (Syntopicon)

The *Syntopicon* (Adler and Gorman, 1990) is a two-volume "idea index"
to the "great ideas" in western thought as collected in the 54-volume set
Great Books of the Western World (1990). The information representations that were processed from these 54 volumes include 1,798 index
terms, approximately 3,000 topics, and review essays of the 102 "great
ideas."

An examination of the *Syntopicon* index indicates that many value-
adding activities were performed during its construction so as to stimu-
late and guide users to the topics in the *Great Books.* Just two examples
of these activities, developing an inventory of terms and outlining topics
relating to the great ideas, are:

Value-adding Activities	Values Added	Examples of Information Representations
Developing an inventory of 1,798 terms to facilitate use of the *Syntopicon* as a reference book	Comprehensiveness, precision, unity, continuity, linkage, selectivity, relevancy, universality, and convenience	Terms: for example, **Value** (econ.): *see* Labor 6*d*; Wealth 4*a*, 4*d*, 6*d*(2)
Outlining 3,000 topics related to the "great ideas" in the *Great Books* and assembling references to them	Comprehensiveness, unity, intelligibility, order, relevancy, convenience	Topics and references: for example, for the term "Labor:" 6*d*. **The natural wages of labor and the labor theory of value 35:** Locke: *Civil Government.*

Value-adding Translating

Translators produce their information representations of documents in the form of full or abridged translations into or from one or more languages. One such translator, Ted Crump, at the National Institutes of Health (NIH) Library Translation Unit, furnishes written, recorded, and oral translations to the NIH scientific community and to the Physician to the Congress. Crump keeps a diary of the information processing steps that he takes to solve nonroutine language translation problems (Cremmins, 1984). Two extracts from his diary illustrate some of the values that he thus adds to his translations.

Problem	Solution
Spelling of instrument type (spektrofotometr "Cilford-2400-2")	Suspected a misspelling. Looked in the *Guide to Scientific Instruments*. Came up dry. Then looked in the latest 5-year set of *SCI Index*. In permuterms under "spectrophotometer" was an entry "Gilford." Looked up author in author section. Title of article referred to "Gilford spectrophotometer." [Values added: accuracy, reliability, precision. E.C.]

| Verification of eponym | Traced a reference given in a Russian-language article to the primary journal article and found that "McLafferty rearrangement" is the correct English for the Russian "peregruppirovka [literally, regrouping] Mak-Lafferti." [Values added: accuracy, reliability, precision. E.C.] |

CONNECTIVE READING AND VALUE-ADDING PROCESSING OF ABSTRACTS

Connective reading for value adding is the first quality check of the draft abstract. By screening out errors in style and content at the source, the abstractor allows reviewers and editors to be more productive while they further refine the quality of the abstract. Connective reading is also beneficial in identifying questions or problems of style that either may be resolved independently by the abstractor or may be brought to the attention of an editor or reviewer. Further, the act of connective reading for value adding reinforces the abstractor's understanding of the rules for abstracting.

Similar to Nozick's (1989) definition of the value of "things," the thing that is an abstract also has a value of its own, an intrinsic value. Intrinsically valuable abstracts should contain a diversity of information that the abstractor selects from the document being abstracted. The diverse information that is selected can be unified organically in the abstract by formatting. The information processing values intrinsic to abstracts may include unity, diversity, coherence, conciseness, brevity, clarity, and consistency. Rules for value-adding abstracting are presented and illustrated in Chapters 12 and 13.

CHAPTER 11

Connective (Value-to-Meaning) Reading: 2. Meaning

meaning 2. That which is intended to be or actually is expressed or indicated. . .b. That which a speaker or writer intends to express; the intended sense of (a person's) words. (p. 522)

—*The Oxford English Dictionary* (1989)

The noun "meaning" has many definitions. The one cited above is the second of six definitions given in the second edition of *The Oxford English Dictionary* (1989). Of the six definitions, this one explains best how "meaning" is used in this text. Therefore, in this chapter, it will be the base for three postulated definitions for meaning in abstracting. The first of these definitions reads:

meaning (abstracting). The abstractor's attempt to ensure that, within the constraints of the time and space allotted to prepare it, as much as possible of what the writer intended to express or indicate in the document being abstracted, and the intended sense of his/her words, have been represented in the abstract.

PSYCHOLOGICAL MEANING-MAKING PROCESSES

> Now let me tell you first what I and my friends thought the [cognitive] revolution was about back there in the late 1950s. It was, we thought, an all-out effort to establish meaning as the central concept of psychology—not stimuli and responses, not overtly observable behavior, not biological drives and their transformation, but meaning. . . . Its aim was to discover and to describe formally the meanings that human beings created out of their encounters with the world, and then to propose hypotheses about what meaning-making processes were implicated. (Bruner, 1990, p. 2)

I acted only as a curious bystander at the "cognitive revolution" that the psychologist Jerome Bruner mentions began in the late 1950s. Yet, I still note a bit of relevant meaning in Bruner's statement for extracting into the second postulated definition of the role of meaning in abstracting:

> **meaning (abstracting).** The abstractor's attempt to ensure that, within the constraints of the time and space allotted to prepare it, as much as possible of what the writer intended to express or indicate in the document being abstracted, and the intended sense of his/her words, have been represented in the abstract. The meaning-making processes draw on the abstractor's problem-solving and decision-making skills, such as reasoning, judging, deducting, inducting, extrapolating, analyzing, and synthesizing.

PHILOSOPHICAL MEANING-MAKING PROCESSES

In Chapter 10, before defining the importance of the value-adding process during abstracting, Nozick's (1989) philosophical explanations and meditations on the evaluative dimension of "value," particularly intrinsic value, were examined briefly. Now the relevance to abstracting of what he has written about a second evaluative dimension, "meaning," will be examined. An extract from the "Value and Meaning" chapter of Nozick's book serves as a good starting point:

> Value is not the only relevant evaluative dimension. We also want our lives and our existence to have meaning. . . . About any

given thing, however wide, it seems we can stand back and ask what its meaning is. To find a meaning for it, then, we seem driven to find a link with yet another thing beyond its boundaries. . . . We need not look beyond something to find its (intrinsic) value, whereas we do have to look beyond a thing to discover its meaning. . . . The greater the link, the closer, the more forceful, the more intense and extensive it is, the greater the meaning gotten. The tighter the connection with value, the greater the meaning. (pp. 168–169)

From this extract, three full and one fragment of Nozick's sentences are salient to the third version of the definition of meaning in abstracting:

1. About any given thing, however wide, it seems we can stand back and ask what its meaning is.

2. To find a meaning for it, then, we seem driven to find a link with yet another thing beyond its boundaries.

3. The greater the link, the closer, the more forceful, the more intense and extensive it is, the greater the meaning gotten.

4. The tighter the connection with value, the greater the meaning.

With Nozick's thoughts in mind, a third and final version of the definition of meaning in abstracting will be constructed:

> **meaning (abstracting).** The abstractor's attempt to ensure that, within the constraints of the time and space allotted to prepare it, as much as possible of what the writer intended to express or indicate in the document being abstracted, and the intended sense of his/her words, have been represented in the abstract. The meaning-making processes draw on the abstractor's problem-solving and decision-making skills, such as reasoning, judging, deducting, inducting, extrapolating, analyzing, and synthesizing. During the second part of connective reading for abstracting, after as much intrinsic value as possible has been added to the draft abstract during the first part, the abstractor now seeks to make the greatest possible meaning out of it by connecting it closely and tightly with the relevant to abstracting information elements in the document being abstracted.

MEANING-MAKING PROCESSES IN ABSTRACTING DURING CONNECTIVE READING

Three meaning-making processes during connective reading for abstracting are:

GENERAL

1. Looking beyond the value-added draft abstract back to the document being abstracted to reconnect with its sources of relevant information (as applicable, on purpose, methods, results or findings, and conclusions or recommendations) to discover if the fullest possible meaningfulness has been obtained from these sources.

ABSTRACTORS FOR ABSTRACTING AND INDEXING SERVICES

1. Further tightening the connection of meaning to the intrinsic value of the draft abstract by recalling from memory or scanning the written guidelines of the abstracting service, then reviewing the abstract to ensure that it fully conforms with them.

2. Intensifying and extending the linkage of value to meaning still further by consulting with other abstractors, editors, technical reviewers, or subject experts, as available and appropriate, to obtain their advice on solving any remaining problems with the style and content of the draft abstract.

Time and availability of human resources permitting, the fulfillment of some or all of these steps should add at least some of the following attributes of meaningfulness to the completed final version of the abstract: readability, pithyness, representativeness, intelligibility, expressiveness, and forcefulness (when active voice is used, if feasible).

CHAPTER 12

Connective Reading for
Sample Abstract A

. . . And so
I say unto you: beware the right margin
Which is unjustified; the left
Is justified and can take care of itself
But what is in between expands and flaps . . . (p. 42)

—JOHN ASHBERY (1963)

Responsive-to-inventive reading versions of sample abstracts A and B
were written and discussed in Chapters 8 and 9. The abstracts are probably longer, if not better, versions than might have been written routinely
by the author or information processing abstractors, because extra time
and effort were put into writing them so as to make them good illustrations. Nevertheless, there is still much that can be done to improve the
style and content of these abstracts.

Partly true to the warning in Ashbery's poem, although the right margins are justified, in between the margins there are definitely some over-
expanded extracts from the text of the sample articles, as well as sentences that contain words and phrases that ambiguously flap out of
sequence or out of context. These samples, however, can be made into
best-quality abstracts by applying the rules of connective (value-to-
meaning) reading, which will take care of the "tucking in" and "smooth-

ing out" of the editorial flaps that were introduced during the preceding responsive-to-inventive reading phase for the writing of the draft abstracts.

RULES FOR CONNECTIVE READING

There are five rules for the self-editing of draft abstracts via connective reading—two for value adding and three for meaning making. Normally, experienced abstractors should have no difficulty applying most of the rules simultaneously during a single analytical reading of their draft abstracts. Novice abstractors are advised to follow the rules separately in sequence. The rules should take experienced abstractors only one to three minutes to apply .

INTRINSIC VALUE ADDING

Rule 1. Is the abstract properly structured and unified?

Rule 2. Is the content of the abstract coherent and concise?

MEANING MAKING

Rule 3. After scanning the text of the document being abstracted, is it clear that the fullest amount of meaning feasible has been represented in the draft abstract?

Rule 4. Does this abstract conform fully with standard abstracting guidelines or those of the sponsoring abstracting service, journal publisher, or data base vendor?

Rule 5. Are there any other problems with the style or content of the draft abstract that might be resolved expediently by consulting with other abstractors, editors, technical reviewers, or subject experts, as available and appropriate?

CONNECTIVE READING FOR SAMPLE ABSTRACT A

The five rules for connective reading will now be applied to the sample abstract of the book review, which was originally published in *Fortune*. First, I will reproduce the draft version of Sample Abstract A from Chapter 8:

The use of systems-analysis techniques and computer modeling as described by Jay W. Forrester in his book *Urban Dynamics* is evaluated. The interrelationships of public policy and financing, taxes, municipal expenditures, employment, housing, and popula-
5   tion mobility are discussed. The effects of land supply and use are also considered. The reviewer concludes that many of the urban management policies proposed in *Urban Dynamics* are inadequate or unrealistic. The significance of taxes and pragmatic financing of urban-renewal programs is overemphasized, and the cost of de-
10 molishing low-income housing and the potential for using vacant lands beyond city limits are overlooked. Responsibilities and functions of local governments should be redistributed to avoid pursuance of narrow self-interests. The reviewer recommends that funding from nonlocal sources should be used to reduce municipal
15 taxes rather than to increase municipal expenditures.

Is this draft abstract properly structured and unified in accordance with Rule 1 of connective reading for abstracting?   No, it is not. The sentence that begins on line 11 with the words "Responsibilities and functions" is presented within the reviewer's conclusions about or criticisms of the book *Urban Dynamics*. But it is, in fact, a recommendation of the reviewer not a conclusion or criticism. Therefore, it should be relocated as the final sentence after the present final one that begins with the words "The reviewer recommends."

Is this abstract coherent and concise, as called for by Rule 2? Hardly. There is much room for improvement through further connective self-editing. Rewording and shortening the first sentence would make for smoother reading. There are almost always opportunities to improve the conciseness of draft abstracts. In this one, at least one needless word can be eliminated from each sentence. The elimination process and the other editing changes are shown below by the use of editing symbols:

The use of systems-analysis techniques and computer modeling as
~~described by~~ Jay W. Forrester ~~in his book~~ *Urban Dynamics* is

evaluated. The interrelationships of public policy and financing,

taxes, municipal expenditures, employment, housing, ~~and~~ population mobility ~~are discussed. The effects of~~ *and* land supply and use are ~~also~~ considered. The reviewer concludes that many of the urban management policies proposed ~~in Urban Dynamics~~ are inadequate or unrealistic, ~~The significance of~~ tax*ation* and pragmatic financing of urban renewal programs *are* overemphasized, and the cost of demolishing low-income housing and the potential for using vacant *rural* lands ~~beyond city limits~~ are overlooked. Responsibilities and functions of local governments should be redistributed to avoid *emphasizing* ~~pursuance of narrow~~ self-interests. The reviewer recommends that funding from nonlocal sources should be used to reduce municipal taxes rather than to increase municipal expenditures.

By rapidly reviewing the content of the draft abstract against the full text of the document being abstracted in an attempt to make further meaning for it (Rule 3), one other reviewer's criticism was identified that should add additional meaning to the abstract: "No explicit mention of reciprocal urban and suburban effects is made in Forrester's systems analysis." After the above editing and the addition of this sentence, the resulting abstract now reads:

> The use of systems-analysis techniques and computer modeling as proposed in Jay W. Forrester's *Urban Dynamics* is evaluated. The interrelationships of public policy and financing, taxes, municipal expenditures, employment, housing, population mobility, and land supply and use are considered. The reviewer concludes that many of the urban management policies proposed are inadequate or unrealistic; taxation and pragmatic financing of urban renewal programs are overemphasized, and the cost of demolishing low-income housing and the potential for using vacant rural lands are overlooked. No explicit mention of reciprocal urban and suburban effects is made in Forrester's systems analysis. The reviewer rec-

ommends that funding from nonlocal sources should be used to reduce municipal taxes rather than to increase municipal expenditures. Responsibilities and functions of local governments should be redistributed to avoid emphasizing self-interests.

Finally, if the abstracting service for which this abstract is assumed to have been written had a strict limitation of 125 words or less for its abstracts, at least 8 words would have to be deleted in accordance with Rule 4 of connective reading, since it now contains 133 words. Accordingly, the final sentence of the revised version probably would be deleted.

COMPUTER-PRODUCED ABSTRACT OF SAMPLE ARTICLE A

Sample Article A was also abstracted as part of a dissertation research study by Mathis (1972), using a test automatic-abstracting system. This abstract will be discussed in Chapter 16.

CHAPTER 13

Connective Reading for Sample Abstract B

Do:

scan the document purposefully for key facts

slant the abstract to your audience

tell what was found

tell why the work was done

tell how the work was done

place findings early in the topical sentence

put details in succeeding sentences

place general statements last

separate relatively independent subjects

differentiate experiment from hypothesis

be informative but brief

be exact, concise, and unambiguous

use short, complete sentences

Dont:

change the meaning of the original

comment on or interpret the document

mention earlier work

include detailed experimental results

describe details for conventional apparatus

mention future work

begin abstracts with stock phrases

use involved phraseology

use questionable jargon

waste words by stating the obvious

say the same thing two ways

use noun form of verbs

over-use synonyms

use a choppy, telegraphic style

—B. H. WEIL; I. ZAREMBER; and H. OWEN (1963b, p. 131)

93

HINTS FOR WRITING GOOD READER-ORIENTED INFORMATIVE ABSTRACTS

The above *do*'s and *don't*'s for "reader-oriented" abstracts (similar to "findings-oriented" abstracts, see Glossary and Chapter 14), which were compiled by Weil, Zarember, and Owen (1963b), are presented here to show a related set of proven guidelines for adding value and making meaning during abstracting. Most of their "hints" for writing good reader- or findings-oriented abstracts are also applicable to the writing of the purpose-oriented abstracts discussed in this book. In fact, the development and use of good analytical reading and thinking skills, in combination with acceptable writing and editing skills that are amenable to improvement and adherence to rules and conventions for abstracting, should enable most individuals to become good abstractors no matter what type of abstract is called for.

CONNECTIVE READING FOR SAMPLE ABSTRACT B

The draft version of Sample Abstract B conforms well with the first three rules for connective (value-to-meaning) reading: It is properly structured and unified, the content is coherent and fairly concise, and a full amount of meaning has been represented from the document being abstracted. But it does not necessarily conform to Rule 4 (see Chapter 12); that is, it does violate at least one recommendation on the preferred length of abstracts. The *American National Standard for Writing Abstracts* (ANSI, 1979) suggests that abstracts for most papers and portions of monographs be kept to fewer than 250 words. Sample Abstract B contains well over 300 words. The deletion of most of three of the sentences containing detailed information on results, four of the sentences that elaborate on the primary conclusions of the study, and other minor deletions will reduce the size of the abstract by more than 100 words, to a total that is much closer to the 250 words recommended in the standard. The original version of Sample Abstract B follows, with the deleted materials underlined.

The effects of oxygen atom addition to olefins on epoxide configuration rearrangements and migration of hydrogen and methyl and

ethyl groups were studied at 90°K <u>by using gas-liquid chromatog-</u>
<u>raphy.</u> *Cis-trans* isomerism in straight-chain, internal olefins and
resulting epoxide compounds was determined. *Cis-* and *trans-*
epoxide, aldehyde, and ketone product-yields were calculated, as
well as ketone and epoxide product-yield ratios for the addition of
$O(^3P)$ to *cis-* and *trans-*2-butene, 2-pentene, 3-hexane, and 4-
octene and *cis-* and *trans-*3,4-dimethyl-3-hexene (DMH) and 3-
ethyl-2-methyl-2-pentene (MEP), respectively. Comparison of the
*trans-*epoxide to ketone ratios from the *cis-* vs. the *trans-*olefin indicates that these ratios diverged with increasing size of the olefin.
Reactions of larger olefins were more stereospecific; <u>*cis-*3-hexene</u>
<u>gave about 2.5 times as much *cis-*3,4-epoxyhexane as the *trans-*</u>
<u>epoxide. *Trans-*olefin compounds produced epoxides containing</u>
<u>90–97%) of the *trans* form, resulting in a 50:1 ratio for the *trans-*</u>
<u>epoxide/aldehyde compounds from the *trans* complex. The *trans-*</u>
<u>epoxide/ketone ratio obtained from the *cis-* as compared to the</u>
<u>*trans-*olefin showed the largest difference with 4-octene.</u> Besides
3,4-epoxy-3,4-dimethylhexane, oxygen addition using DMH gave
4,4-dimethyl-3-hexanone (I) and 3-ethyl-3-methyl-2-pentanone (II)
ketones, depending on whether the methyl or ethyl group migrated. <u>The reaction gave no other products.</u> Using MEP, the same
two ketones were produced as from *cis-* and *trans-*DMH; but ketone
(I) resulted from methyl and ethyl group migration, starting with
DMH and MEP, respectively. Opposite migrations produced ketone
II. Results suggest that retention of configuration of products is
dependent on olefin chain length, and that reaction of oxygen atoms at low temperature is more stereospecific with *trans-*olefins.
<u>Stereotransformation of the transition intermediate requires a 180°</u>
<u>rotation of one of the carbon atoms of the double bond with its at-</u>
<u>tached groups about the modified olefinic bond, which occurs with</u>
<u>the *cis-*olefins. Stereotransformation is a factor of rates of ring</u>
<u>closure and rearrangement leading to final products, compared to</u>
<u>the *cis-trans* interchange in the complex. Ring closure probably is</u>
<u>independent of olefin size.</u> Concerted rearrangement involving
oxygen localization and group migration requires electronic and
spatial reorganization. Addition of ground-state, triplet oxygen to
singlet-state olefin to give singlet-state products probably requires
a relaxation process. <u>Group migration probably involves a tran-</u>
<u>sient bridging of the bond carbon pair, and intermediate relaxation</u>
<u>to final products could involve steric effects.</u>

The revised shorter version of Sample Abstract B follows.

The effects of oxygen atom addition to olefins on epoxide configuration rearrangements and migration of hydrogen and methyl and ethyl groups were studied at 90°K. *Cis-trans* isomerism in straight-chain, internal olefins and resulting epoxide compounds was determined. *Cis-* and *trans*-epoxide, aldehyde, and ketone product-yields were calculated, as well as ketone and epoxide product-yield ratios for the addition of O(^{3}P) to *cis-* and *trans*-2-butene, 2-pentene, 3-hexane, and 4-octene and *cis-* and *trans*-3,4-dimethyl-3-hexene (DMH) and 3-ethyl-2-methyl-2-pentene (MEP), respectively. Comparison of the *trans*-epoxide to ketone ratios from the *cis-* vs. the *trans*-olefin indicates that these ratios diverged with increasing size of the olefin. Reactions of larger olefins were more stereospecific. Besides 3,4-epoxy-3,4-dimethylhexane, oxygen addition using DMH gave 4,4-dimethyl-3-hexanone (I) and 3-ethyl-3-methyl-2-pentanone (II) ketones, depending on whether the methyl or ethyl group migrated. Using MEP, the same two ketones were produced as from *cis-* and *trans*-DMH; but ketone (I) resulted from methyl and ethyl group migration, starting with DMH and MEP, respectively. Opposite migrations produced ketone II. Results suggest that retention of configuration of products is dependent on olefin chain length, and that reaction of oxygen atoms at low temperature is more stereospecific with *trans*-olefins. Concerted rearrangement involving oxygen localization and group migration requires electronic and spatial reorganization. Addition of ground-state, triplet oxygen to singlet-state olefin to give singlet-state products probably requires a relaxation process.

Incidentally, in accordance with Rule 5 (see Chapter 12) of connective reading (*Are there any other problems with the style or content of the draft abstract that might be resolved expediently by consulting with other abstractors, editors, technical reviewers, or subject experts, as available or appropriate?*), two chemists were consulted during the preparation of this abstract.

COMPUTER-PRODUCED ABSTRACT OF
SAMPLE ARTICLE B

Sample Article B also was abstracted as part of a dissertation research study by Mathis (1972) using a test automatic abstracting system. This abstract will be discussed in Chapter 16.

PART V

MORE EDITING AND REVISING OF ABSTRACTS, AND SOME THOUGHTS ON THE THOUGHT PROCESSES DURING DOCUMENTAL INFORMATION PROCESSING

INDICATIVE ABSTRACT

Six precomposed abstracts are edited using a modified "checklist of the writing process." Four sample author or computational abstracts are edited and revised. Also, the thought processes associated with documental information processing are examined.

99

CHAPTER 14

Assisted Invitations to Editing of Sample Abstracts

This book . . . offers not rules and exhortations but assisted invitations to students of composition to discover what they are trying to do and thereby how to do it. (p. 2)

—ANN E. BERTHOFF (1978)

Thus far, this book *has offered* many "rules and exhortations" on how to compose abstracts and "assisted invitations" (incentives) to follow the process during the composition of two sample abstracts. Before presenting a few rules and exhortations on developing and maintaining cooperative relationships among abstractors, editors, managers, and users of abstracts in Part VI of this book, I will present here additional, but less formal, assisted invitations to examine completed sample abstracts.

These abstracts will be edited to improve their intrinsic value, but not their meaning, since they were not reviewed against the documents from which they were abstracted.

SAMPLE PRECOMPOSED ABSTRACTS

In her introduction to *Forming, Thinking, Writing: the Composing Imagination*, Berthoff (1978) observes that most teachers agree that "the

101

fundamentals of composing have to be presented, analyzed, demonstrated over and over again." Accordingly, the six sample precomposed abstracts that follow are shown in three versions:

1. Unedited purpose-oriented form
2. Edited purpose-oriented form
3. Findings-oriented version of the edited purpose-oriented abstract

The first versions of the six precomposed abstracts are analyzed briefly by using a modification of Brusaw, Alred, and Oliu's (1993) "Checklist of the Writing Process," which follows:

1. Replace abstract words with concrete ones
2. Check for appropriate word choice
3. Achieve conciseness
4. Check for unity and coherence
5. Check for clarity
6. Eliminate awkwardness
7. Check sentence construction and achieve sentence variety
(pp. xviii–xix)

Sample 1. Informative abstract composed from a translated report on occupational health therapy.

a. Unedited purpose-oriented form:

Observations on the *skin tumors*[1] in workers exposed to coal tar in a charcoal briquette factory were reported. Six of 10 cases of *tar tumors*[2] occurred inside the factory and 4 occurred on the outside. *All of the skin tumors involved the face.*[3] The principal localizations in decreasing order of incidence, were the nose (*8 localizations*[3]), the eyelids (*7 localizations*[3]), the lips (*4 localizations*[3]), and the ears (*2 localizations*[3]). *The tumors appeared after widely varying periods of exposure, ranging from 1 year to 43 years.*[3] The histologic variety of these tumors was independent of the duration of exposure. *In half the cases*[1], there were multiple tumors. Three major types of tumors revealed by histologic results were keratoacanthoma, papilloma, and epithelioma. *All these tumors were curable with the therapeutic methods now available: electrocoagulation and radiotherapy.[3] In comparing the delay in appearance of tumors as a function of job assignment, it was noted that the 5 patients showing tumors within the first 10 years of exposure were those most highly exposed to the coal tar[3]*

---

[1]Replace abstract words with concrete ones. [2]Check for appropriate word choice. [3]Achieve conciseness.

b. Edited purpose-oriented form:

Ten case reports are presented of facial skin tumors in workers in a charcoal briquette factory who were exposed to coal tar. Six of the incidences occurred in workers inside the factory and four occurred in workers outside. Principal localizations of the tumors were the nose, eyelids, lips, and ears, with 8, 7, 4, and 2 localizations, respectively. The tumors appeared after periods of exposure of 1 to 43 years. Histologically, the three major types of tumors identified (keratoacanthoma, papilloma, and epithelioma) were not exposure related. Five of the workers had multiple tumors. The five workers who had tumors within the first 10 years of exposure were among those who were most highly exposed to the coal tar. All tumors responded to electrocoagulation and radiotherapy.

c. Findings-oriented version of the edited purpose-oriented abstract (b):

Facial skin tumors were identified in 10 workers exposed to coal tar in a charcoal briquette factory. Six of the incidences occurred in workers inside the factory and four occurred in workers outside. Principal localizations of the tumors were the nose, eyelids, lips, and ears, with 8, 7, 4, and 2 localizations, respectively. The tumors appeared after periods of exposure of 1 to 43 years. Histologically, the three major types of tumors identified (keratoacanthoma, papilloma, and epithelioma) were not exposure related. Five of the workers had multiple tumors. The five workers who had tumors within the first 10 years of exposure were among those who were most highly exposed to the coal tar. All tumors responded to electrocoagulation and radiotherapy.

Sample 2. Informative abstract composed from an article on drug abuse and personality.

a. Unedited purpose-oriented form:

The *personality characteristics*[4] of adolescent drug abusers were *studied in a comparison*[3] of an adolescent drug-abusing group and *an adolescent nonabusing group*[3] from *middle and upper middle classes.*[5] *The variable of sex was also studied.*[4] The Minnesota Multiphasic Personality Inventory (MMPI) *was used to evaluate personalties.*[4] *Results showed that there were certain personality characteristics which distinguished adolescent drug abusers from nonabusers.*[3] Drug abusers were more nonconforming, tended to reject social conventions, and lacked the ability to form satisfactory emotional relationships. *No difference*[2] was found between male and female users based on MMPI scales.

---

[2]Check for appropriate word choice. [3]Achieve conciseness. [4]Check for unity and coherence. [5]Check for clarity.

b. Edited purpose-oriented form:

Personality characteristics and sex of adolescent drug-abusing and nonabusing groups from middle- and upper-middle-class families were compared. The Minnesota Multiphasic Personality Inventory (MMPI) was administered to both groups. Drug abusers were more nonconforming, tended to reject social conventions, and failed to form satisfactory emotional relationships. The MMPI revealed no significant differences between male and female drug users.

c. Findings-oriented version of the edited purpose-oriented abstract (b):

Drug abusers were more nonconforming than nonabusers, tended to reject social conventions, and failed to form satisfactory emotional relationships, according to results obtained with middle- and upper-middle-class adolescents administered the Minnesota Multiphasic Personality Inventory. No significant differences were found between male and female drug users.

Sample 3. Informative abstract composed from a study in psychology.

a. Unedited purpose-oriented form:

The problems of the child without a family and the best methods of providing for the needs felt by this child from infancy onward[3] are discussed. *The needs are described as simple:*[4] The child should be welcomed, loved, given a feeling of "belonging." *The best solution of the child's problem is early permanent adoption by one family.*[4] *If this proves impossible,*[3] successive foster-home situations should be avoided. *Careful psychological examinations and advice should be accorded the child*[5] when a change of environment from foster home to foster home, or from institution to institution, is required. *If the child has suffered from lack of the above, his troubles should be identified and treated quickly.*[5] The child should be taught early to retain, regain, or develop self-esteem. He should *always*[2] have a sole advisor *who can help him make and decide on necessary changes*[5] and who has his full confidence.

-----

[2]Check for appropriate word choice. [3]Achieve conciseness. [4]Check for unity and coherence. [5]Check for clarity.

b. Edited purpose-oriented form:

The rearing of familyless children from infancy to adulthood was studied. The child should be welcomed, loved, and given a feeling of belonging, preferably through early permanent adoption by one family. Placement in successive foster homes should be avoided. Psychological examinations and constructive advice should be given when children change foster homes or institutions. Problem children should be identified and treated quickly. Familyless children should be taught early to retain, regain, or develop self-esteem. A single advisor to help the child adjust and who has his complete confidence should be assigned.

c. *Findings-oriented version of the edited purpose-oriented abstract (b):*

Familyless children should be welcomed, loved, and given a feeling of belonging from infancy to adulthood, preferably through early permanent adoption by one family. Placement in successive foster homes should be avoided. Psychological examinations and constructive advice should be given when children change foster homes or institutions. Problem children should be identified and treated quickly. Familyless children should be taught early to retain, regain, or develop self-esteem. A single advisor to help the child adjust and who has his complete confidence should be assigned.

Sample 4. Informative abstract from a translated epidemiological report on ophthalmology.

a. Unedited purpose-oriented form:

The occurrence of macular hemorrhages and macular holes[2] *in cases of*[3] degenerative myopia was studied in 2511 eyes in 1525 patients *with degenerative myopia*[3] in Kyoto, Japan. Of the total, 1551 were female and 960 were male eyes, *indicating a preference for females.*[3] The number of cases of degenerative myopia increased *in proportion as both age and degree of myopia increased.*[6] Macular hemorrhage was observed *in 114 eyes of which females were 70 and males 44.*[6] A high incidence of macular hemorrhage was observed in the young and in the elderly groups and *was frequently observed in cases of degenerative myopia of low degree,*[5] *suggesting that macular hemorrhage is a complication in the early stages of degenerative myopia.*[3] Macular holes were observed in 182 eyes, *147 of which were of females and only 35 eyes were of males.*[6] Macular holes resulting in retinal detachment were found in 80 female eyes and 11 male eyes. The formation of macular holes was *rarely seen in the young group and its incidence increased in proportion to aging.*[5, 7]

---

[2]Check for appropriate word choice. [3]Achieve conciseness. [5]Check for clarity. [6]Eliminate awkwardness. [7]Check sentence construction and achieve sentence variety.

b. Edited purpose-oriented form:

Macular hemorrhages and vacuoles in degenerative myopia were studied in 2511 eyes in 1525 patients in Kyoto, Japan. The sample comprised 1551 female and 960 male eyes. The number of cases of degenerative myopia increased in proportion to increased age and degree of myopia. Macular hemorrhages were observed in 70 female and 44 male eyes. A high incidence of hemorrhaging was observed in young and elderly patients and in cases of minor degenerative myopia. Macular vacuoles were observed in 147 female and 35 male eyes; vacuoles resulting in retinal detachment were found in 80 female and 11 male eyes. The incidence of vacuoles increased with age. They were rarely seen in younger patients.

c. *Findings-oriented version of the edited purpose-oriented abstract (b):*

Macular hemorrhages and vacuoles were more prevalent in female patients with degenerative myopia. In 1525 patients in Kyoto, Japan, the number of cases of degenerative myopia also increased in proportion to increased age and degree of myopia. Macular hemorrhages were observed in 70 female and 44 male eyes of the 1551 female and 960 male eyes in the sample. A high incidence of hemorrhaging was observed in young and elderly patients and in cases of minor degenerative myopia. Macular vacuoles were observed in 147 female and 35 male eyes; vacuoles resulting in retinal detachment were found in 80 female and 11 male eyes. The incidence of vacuoles increased with age. They were rarely seen in younger patients.

Sample 5. Informative abstract composed from an environmental science study.

a. *Unedited purpose-oriented form:*

The sources of potentially hazardous elements contained in urban roadway[2,3] were studied. A 648-gram sample of urban roadway dust was subdivided according to particle size, density, and ferromagnetic susceptibility and was analyzed for trace elements. Lead and cadmium were extracted from each sample and determined by atomic absorption spectrophotometry. Thirty-three other elements were found in a subsample by instrumental neutron activation analysis. Different methods were used to calculate the sources, then, by summing the source factors over all the samples, to calculate the percentage contribution to the total sample of each source.[3,5] This conclusion was derived: 76 percent (p) soil, 5.0 p cement, 0.3 p salt, 1.5 p automobile-exhaust particles, 7.7 p iron, 7.2 p automobile tire-wear particles, and 2.3 p unaccounted for.[3,5] Statistical analysis was used to come to these conclusions, but the author suggests more detailed graphical presentation and more

extensive fractionization to achieve more accurate results because
resolving power of analysis is insufficient to distinguish between
sources that produce similar physical characteristics.[2,3,5,6]

---

[2]Check for appropriate word choice. [3]Achieve conciseness.
[5]Check for clarity. [6]Eliminate awkwardness.

b. *Edited purpose-oriented form:*

A 648-gram sample representative of roadway dust in a moderately large, nonindustrial urban community was subdivided by particle size, density, and ferromagnetic susceptibility, and
subfractions were analyzed to determine major, minor, and trace
elements. Results were subjected to multivariate statistical analysis to identify and quantify the sources in the sample. The roadway dust sample contained 76.0, 5.0, 0.3, 1.5, 7.7, 7.2, and 2.3
percent of soil, cement, salt, automobile-exhaust particles, iron,
tire-wear particles, and unidentified substances, respectively. The
combined use of statistical and quantitative analyses is recommended when characterizing urban roadway dust.

c. *Findings-oriented version of the edited purpose-oriented ab-stract (b):*

The roadway dust in a 648-gram sample representative of that
from a moderately large, nonindustrial urban community contained 76.0, 5.0, 0.3, 1.5, 7.7, 7.2, and 2.3 percent of soil, cement,
salt, automobile-exhaust particles, iron, tire-wear particles, and
unidentified substances, respectively. The sample had been subdivided by particle size, density, and ferromagnetic susceptibility,
and subfractions had been analyzed to determine major, minor,
and trace elements. Results were subjected to multivariate statistical analysis to identify and quantify the sources in the sample.
The combined use of statistical and quantitative analyses is recommended when characterizing urban roadway dust.

Sample 6. Informative abstract composed from an article on psychology.

a. *Unedited purpose-oriented form:*

The experimental work reported studied the phenomenon[3] *of sug-*
gestibility *under four different forms of suggestion: indirect, auto-,*
hetero-, and conflicting.[3,6] Healthy and ill students and patients,
with and without autogenic training, were *tested with the Body*

Sway Test[6] to measure the effect of the suggestion. *The results were: (a) equally strong effects occurred under all four forms of suggestion; (b) autogenic training affected positive behavior on the Body Sway Test in both healthy and ill students; (c) the negative behavior in the Body Sway Test occurred when autogenic training was lacking; (d) under the conflicting suggestions, the behavior of the female patients was more positive than that of the male patients.*[3, 7]

---

[3]Achieve conciseness. [6]Eliminate awkwardness. [7]Check sentence construction and achieve sentence variety.

b. *Edited purpose-oriented form:*

Suggestibility was measured under indirect, auto-, hetero-, and conflicting forms of suggestion by using the Body Sway Test. Healthy and ill students and patients, with and without autogenic training, were tested. Equally strong effects occurred under all four forms of suggestion. Autogenic training affected positive behavior on the test in both healthy and ill students. Negative behavior in this test occurred when autogenic training was lacking. The behavior of female patients was more positive than that of males under conflicting suggestions.

c. *Findings-oriented version of the edited purpose-oriented abstract (b):*

Equally strong effects of suggestion occurred under indirect, auto-, hetero-, and conflicting forms when the Body Sway Test was given to healthy and ill students and patients, with and without autogenic training. The training affected positive behavior on the test in both healthy and ill students. Negative behavior in this test occurred when autogenic training was lacking. The behavior of female patients was more positive than that of males under conflicting suggestions.

CHAPTER 15

Editing or Revising "Author" Abstracts

*The process of revision, for most students, has not been concerned with finding meaning, but has focused on editing superficial mechanical and grammatical errors to a preconceived and often not clearly understood standard. It is important for students to see revision in a larger context that **includes** editing, but is **not only** a matter of editing.* (p. x)

—DONALD M. MURRAY (1991)

In Chapters 12 and 13, the editing and revising of sample abstracts A and B were discussed as part of the third and final process of reading when writing original abstracts. This chapter and Chapter 16 will be devoted to the editing or revising of abstracts that have not been written by the editor or reviser but by others, without (Chapter 15) or with (Chapter 16) the assistance of computers. Chapter 17 on the role of thinking during documental information processing will then conclude this part of the book.

AUTHOR ABSTRACTS

Author abstracts are herein defined as those that have been written by someone with whom the editor or reviser has no direct contact. These editors or revisers normally work for an abstracting or indexing service, an information analysis center, a data base vendor or publisher, or a library. In this chapter and Chapter 16, all of these organizations or facilities will be referred to collectively as "information systems." When such information systems edit or revise author abstracts, they are obliged to do so in strict compliance with copyright rules.

Most "author abstracts" are, in fact, written by the author or authors of the document. But some of the "author" abstracts that are the object of this discussion actually may have been written by someone other than the author, such as a staff member of a scientific, technical, or scholarly journal, or someone at the office or facility where the original article or report was written. Since the editing or revising processes for the latter are similar and also usually are done without any interaction between their originators and the information system editors, for convenience, these will be assumed to be quasi-author abstracts.

Three versions of the processes used in the editing or revising of two actual, not quasi-, author abstracts will now be illustrated. These versions are of author abstracts that (1) were not changed or were changed slightly, (2) were edited, and (3) were revised, which included significant editing. Although the full texts of the articles for these author abstracts will not be reproduced here, they were on hand and were used during the writing of the revised versions, but not during the preparation of the edited versions.

As with the writing of the sample abstracts that were described in Parts II–IV of this book, during the editing or revising of the sample author abstracts, full attention was given to the processes of adding value and making them more meaningful.

SAMPLE AUTHOR ABSTRACT A

The first author abstract, an indicative one, appeared with Craven's (1991) article, "Graphic Display of Larger Sentence Dependency Structures," in the *Journal of the American Society for Information Science (JASIS)*. The original version of this abstract is shown exactly as it appears in *JASIS*, with the exception of my insertion of the notation (Author Abstract) at the end. This notation is customarily added to such abstracts when they are accessioned into some information systems.

Version 1: indicative—unchanged:

> This article outlines desirable qualities for graphic representation of sentence dependency structures in texts of more than a few sentences in length. Several different approaches prototyped within the TEXNET experimental text structure management system are described, illustrated, and compared. The usefulness of automatic structure simplification and of automatic addition of dummy sentences is noted. (Author Abstract)

Version 2: indicative—edited:

The second version is postulated to have been prepared after the abstract had been selected for editing for inclusion in a hypothetical information system on computational information processing (ISCIP). This abstract was edited in conformance with the assumed principle of the ISCIP data base, that is, striving to add intrinsic value to the abstracts being processed into the system.

> The qualities for graphic representation of sentence dependency structures in texts longer than a few sentences are outlined. Prototyped TEXNET experimental text structure management is discussed, along with automatic structure simplification and the addition of dummy sentences. (Author Abstract, edited)

In agreement with Weil, Zarember, and Owen's (1963b) "Hints for writing good reader-oriented informative abstracts" (reproduced earlier on page 93), the edited abstract was made more concise (per their hint: "Do be exact, concise, and unambiguous") than the original one, without any loss in meaning (their hint: "Don't change the meaning of the original"). One way that conciseness was achieved during editing involved substituting the two words "is discussed," for the five words "are described, illustrated, and compared," at the close of the second sentence in the original abstract, in accordance with their hint "Don't use involved phraseology." Also, in keeping with their hint "Don't begin abstracts with stock phrases," the first sentence was recast to delete the opening stock phrase "This article."

Version 3: indicative–informative—revised:

Assuming that, whenever feasible, the preparation of informative or indicative–informative abstracts is required for the hypothetical ISCIP data base, the edited indicative abstract in Version 2 will now be revised into an indicative–informative abstract. This will be done by making more meaning through a comparison of the content of the edited indicative abstract against the full text of the article being abstracted. Next, relevant informative materials that were discovered during the comparison will be extracted from the text. Secondarily, intrinsic value will be added to the extracts through editing. Three meaning-making passages (A, B, and C below) were extracted from Craven's (1991) text and edited for Version 3:

Textual Extracts

A. The TEXNET prototype employs a fairly simple intermediate representation, consisting of the sentences of the original text plus links representing sentence dependencies. (22 words)

A later sentence in a text is considered to be dependent on an earlier sentence if the later sentence needs information from the earlier sentence in order to be understood. (30 words)

Production of a summary is viewed as a process of extraction of sentences from the source. (16 words)

B. Desirable Qualities in Graphic Displays: (1) Clear indication of all direct dependency relationships between sentences. (2) Reflection of the order of the original text. (3) Indication of the content of each sentence. (4) Easy designation of each sentence. (5) Quick generation of the display from basic information about sentences and links, and quick regeneration

Edited Textual Extracts

The TEXNET prototype uses an intermediate representation of the original textual sentences plus links to reveal their dependencies. (18 words)

A later textual sentence is dependent on an earlier one if it needs information from the latter to be understood. (19 words)

The summarizing process amounts to extracting sentences from the source. (10 words)

Desirable qualities in graphic displays include (1) a clear indication of all direct dependency relationships between sentences; (2) a reflection of the order of the original text; and (3) an indication of the content of each sentence.

[NOTE: Because of assumed limitations in the length of abstracts for the postulated ISCIP system, only three of

if a sentence or link changes. (6) Capability of being displayed, at least in part, while part of the full text is being displayed or edited. (7) Functionality for texts up to 100 sentences at least.

C. As already pointed out elsewhere . . . , given certain assumptions about how the structure information is to be used, some polyhierarchical structures can be simplified to monohierarchies.

Another method of structural modfication involves the use of virtual, or dummy, sentences. This method is possible if two or more sentences are directly dependent on the same two or more other sentences.

Automatic structure simplification and addition of virtual sentences seem to be useful automatic techniques for improving the readability of graphic representations of larger sentence dependency structures.

the seven "desirable qualities in graphic displays" that were described in Craven's text and listed in the left-hand column were selected for editing into the edited textual extract.]

Automatic structure simplification (e.g., from poly- to monohierarchies) and the addition of virtual (dummy) sentences, when two or more sentences are directly dependent on the same two or more other sentences, may improve the readability of graphic representations of larger sentence dependency structures.

[NOTE: This edited textual extract results from consolidating the information in the three textual sentences listed under "C" in the left-hand column.]

The resulting indicative–informative version (3) of the author's abstract, which was revised using valued-added editing and meaning-making revision, is shown below, preceded by the original (1) and edited indicative (2) versions.

Version 1: indicative—unchanged:

This article outlines desirable qualities for graphic representation of sentence dependency structures in texts of more than a few sentences in length. Several different approaches prototyped within the TEXNET experimental text structure management system are described, illustrated and compared. The usefulness of automatic structure simplification and of automatic addition of dummy sentences is noted. (Author Abstract)

Version 2: indicative—edited:

The qualities for graphic representation of sentence dependency structures in texts longer than a few sentences are outlined. Prototyped TEXNET experimental text structure management is discussed, along with automatic structure simplification and the addition of dummy sentences. (Author Abstract, edited)

Version 3: indicative–informative—revised:

The qualities for graphic representation of sentence dependency structures in texts longer than a few sentences are outlined. Prototyped experimental text structure management is discussed, along with automatic structure simplification and the addition of dummy sentences. The TEXNET prototype uses an intermediate representation of the original textual sentences plus links to reveal their dependencies. A later textual sentence is dependent on an earlier one if it needs information from the latter to be understood. The summarizing process amounts to extracting sentences from the source. Desirable qualities in graphic displays include a clear indication of all direct dependency relationships between sentences; a reflection of the order of the original text; and an indication of the content of each sentence. Automatic structure simplification (e.g., from poly- to monohierarchies) and the addition of virtual (dummy) sentences when two or more sentences are directly dependent on two or more other sentences may improve the readability of graphic representations of larger sentence dependency structures. (Author Abstract, revised)

In Version 3, the five sentences of edited extracts from the text that were added to the three sentences of the original abstract add informative (meaningful) statements on the author's main themes: sentence dependency structures, automatic structure simplification, and the addition of virtual (dummy) sentences. The additions are intended to assist further the users of the ISCIP data base in determining whether they would like to acquire the full text of Craven's (1991) article.

SAMPLE AUTHOR ABSTRACT B

Sample Author Abstract B is from Kuhlen's (1984) paper, "Some Similarities and Differences Between Intellectual and Machine Text Understanding for the Purpose of Abstracting." His indicative–informative abstract for the paper is shown intact below, with the minor exceptions that a hyphen was removed between the words "West" and "Germany" in the original first sentence; hyphens were inserted between "surface" and "oriented" and "high" and "quality" in the original second sentence; and a comma was inserted in the last sentence, in accordance with the assumed style guidelines of the ISCIP information system.

Version 1: indicative–informative—slightly changed:

The analysis of a set of intellectual abstracting rules taken from actual practice in working systems in West Germany leads to the conclusion that, so far, there is no way of real machine simulation of intellectual text abstracting capacity, due to the significant differences in machine and human analysis and condensation techniques. But, on the other hand, there is no evidence for the traditional belief that surface-oriented text analysis procedures, mainly statistically oriented, can produce high-quality abstracting. There is a need for knowledge-based text analysis and processing (inferencing and transformation). As a result of the survey of abstracting rules, requirements for an automatic abstracting system are formulated. (Author Abstract)

The edited version of this abstract for the ISCIP information system reads as follows:

Version 2: indicative–informative—edited:

Analysis of abstracting rules for German working systems reveals that no method exists, as yet, for real machine simulation of intellectual text abstracting, owing to differences in machine and human analysis and condensation techniques. Also, evidence is lacking for the belief that surface (primarily statistical) textual analysis can produce high-quality abstracts. Knowledge-based textual analysis and processing (inferencing and transformation) are needed. Abstracting rule-based requirements are formulated for an automatic abstracting system. (Author Abstract, edited)

Version 2 of Sample Author Abstract B was primarily edited with Weil, Zarember, and Owen's (1963b) hint for writing good informative abstracts in mind—"be informative but brief." Here, this approach led to a reduction of 36 words between versions 1 and 2 (107 and 71 words, respectively, while counting hyphenated words as one word in both versions).

For Version 3, the first step in revising this edited author abstract will be to substitute for some of the author's terms others that are assumed to be more consistent with the vocabulary of the ISCIP information system:

For author's terms	Substitute
(in the first sentence)	
working systems	operational information systems
real machine simulation	authentic computer simulation
intellectual text abstracting	human abstracting
machine. . .analysis	computer-aided. . .analysis
condensation	representation
(in the last sentence)	
automatic abstracting	computational abstracting

The resulting partially revised abstract now reads as follows:

Version 3: indicative–informative—partially revised:

Analysis of abstracting rules for German operational information systems reveals that no method exists, as yet, for authentic computer simulation of human abstracting, owing to differences in computer-aided and human analysis and representation techniques. Also, evidence is lacking to support the belief that surface (primarily statistical) textual analysis can produce high-quality abstracts. Knowledge-based textual analysis and processing (inferencing and transformation) are needed. Abstracting rule-based requirements are formulated for a computational abstracting system. (Author Abstract, revised)

The second step in this approximation of the revision process will be a rapid exploratory reading of the full text of the article to discover if there are any more extractable sentences that will make the abstract more meaningful. During the reading, three sections in Kuhlen's (1984) article were identified that contain candidate sentences for expanding the informative content of the author abstract. The themes of these sections result from the author's survey of abstracting rules in terms of general characteristics of abstracts and abstracting, general and specific requirements for human abstracting, and requirements for an "automatic" (computational) system.

It would unduly lengthen the author abstract to include information from all three sections in a balanced way. Therefore, only extracts from the third section will be added to the revised abstract for responsive representation. This section was chosen because it is pertinent to the author's own research with others on two computational abstracting projects, as outlined in his paper. Also, this research is mentioned indirectly in the last sentence of the author's original abstract ("As a result of the survey of abstracting rules, requirements for an automatic abstracting system are formulated."). The original and edited textual extracts from this section are shown below.

Textual Extracts	*Edited Textual Extracts*
. . . we can formulate the following recommendations for the construction of an [automatic] abstracting system	Four abstracting rule-based recommendations for a computational abstracting system are given. These are
1. It should be knowledge based and full text oriented, that means it should be able to transfer the text completely into a knowledge structure and to partition the text into its main and subordinate parts.	1. Transfer text completely into a knowledge structure and partition it into its main and subordinate parts.
2. It should be able to compare text information with the general standard in the field to be covered in order to identify really new results.	2. Compare text with standards in the field covered to identify new results.
3. It should be flexible with respect to different users' needs, that means, the output format should vary significantly both formally and with regard to the content.	3. Fulfill different users' needs with varying output formats.

4. The abstracting system should be embedded into a retrieval system on a full text basis, that means, the highly desirable gradation from very general information about the text to very specific information from the text itself should be realized in one single system.

4. Embed into the full-text retrieval system both broad general information about the text and specific information from the text itself.

The original, edited, and revised versions of Sample Author Abstract B now read as follows:

Original

The analysis of a set of intellectual abstracting rules taken from actual practice in working systems in West Germany leads to the conclusion that, so far, there is no way of real machine simulation of intellectual text abstracting capacity, due to the significant differences in machine and human analysis and condensation techniques. But, on the other hand, there is no evidence for the traditional belief that surface-oriented text analysis procedures, mainly statistically oriented, can produce high-quality abstracting. There is a need for knowledge-based text analysis and processing (inferencing and transformation). As a result of the survey of abstracting rules, requirements for an automatic abstracting system are formulated. (Author Abstract)

Edited

Analysis of abstracting rules for German working systems reveals that no method exists, as yet, for real machine simulation of intellectual text abstracting, owing to differences in machine and human analysis and condensation techniques. Also, evidence is lacking for the belief that surface (primarily statistical) textual analysis can produce high-quality abstracts. Knowledge-based textual analysis and processing (inferencing and transformation) are needed. Abstracting rule-based requirements are formulated for an automatic abstracting system. (Author Abstract, edited)

Revised

Analysis of abstracting rules for German operational information systems reveals that no method exists, as yet, for authentic computer simulation of human abstracting, owing to differences in computer-aided and human analysis and representation techniques. Also, evidence is lacking to support the belief that surface (primarily statistical) textual analysis can produce high-quality abstracts. Knowledge-based textual analysis and processing (inferencing and transformation) are needed. Four abstracting rule-based recommendations for a computational abstracting system are given. These are (1) transfer text completely into a knowledge structure and partition it into its main and subordinate parts, (2) compare text with standards in the field covered to identify new results, (3) fulfill different users' needs with varying output formats, and (4) embed into the full-text retrieval system both broad general information about the text and specific information from the text itself. (Author Abstract, revised)

ELEMENTS OF PROCESSING AUTHOR ABSTRACTS

Thus far in this chapter, a few of the many ways to edit or revise author abstracts for input into information systems have been demonstrated. Three approaches to completing this type of documental information processing were suggested:

1. *No, or minor, editing* (Author Abstract). The information system's editor or abstractor-editor scrutinizes the author abstract and determines whether it has adequate intrinsic value under the guidelines of a particular information system. No changes, or only minor ones to correct wrong spelling, punctuation, or word usage, are deemed necessary before the abstract is approved for forwarding to the next step in the processing cycle.

2. *Editing* (Author Abstract, edited). After scrutinizing the author abstract, the editor or abstractor-editor determines that moderate to significant changes need to be made to add to its intrinsic value. Besides spelling and punctuation, other more significant changes to sentences may be necessary to ensure that the abstract is written in correct, concise, simple, and idiomatic English.

3. *Revising* (Author Abstract, revised). A microcosm of the full abstracting process, the revising of author abstracts may involve not only editing them internally but also comparing them externally against the text of the document being abstracted, with the aim of making more meaning out of them.

CHAPTER 16

Editing or Revising "Computational" Abstracts

When it became technically feasible for computers to process alphabetical as well as numerical symbols, new fields of application were investigated. Machine translation was the first of the language-processing applications, followed by automatic abstracting, automatic indexing and automatic document classification. By analogy to the programs that made it possible for a document to be translated from one language into another, programs were written for the condensation of the contents in the same language. In the first case the concepts and terms had to be matched with foreign language equivalents, in the latter case the most relevant terms had to be selected according to the respective subject vocabulary and reproduced with their contexts. (p. 162)

—WOLFGANG NEDOBITY (1982)

COMPUTATIONAL ABSTRACTING

Nedobity (1982) and many other researchers in information science, linguistics, and computer science identify the attempts to write programs for computerized representation and condensation of the contents of documents into abstracts as "automatic abstracting." Still others label this form of computer processing as "machine abstracting" or "computer-based abstracting." It will be referred to here as "computational abstracting."

I prefer the term computational abstracting, within the broader concept of computational information processing, because it best describes the writing of programs, using computational linguistics, for the computer processing of natural language into abstracts, as opposed to the human writing of abstracts within the broader concept of documental information processing.

Prototype computational abstracting systems generally involve programming the computer to select, reject, or modify sentences electronically from full or partial textual input and to arrange them sequentially for output as abstracts.

In-depth research into computational abstracting began approximately 40 years ago and continues into the 1990s. Although a few promising computational abstracting systems have been developed over the past 40 years, almost none of them has progressed beyond the extracting stage into actual full-scale abstracting.

Zamora and Zamora (1990) reflect 10 years later about an automatic abstracting project for chemical abstracts that did not get beyond the research stage. The aim of the abstracting system, which they co-developed, was to produce abstracts from natural-language text automatically. The abstracting technique relied on rudimentary parsing techniques and semantic categorization.

Some anticipated problems of the project were that:

> There was a lack of machine-readable primary journal data that could be input to the automatic abstracting program . . . . At that time, optical character recognition as a form of data acquisition was not reliable for the different font types that needed to be processed. (p. 184)

> Manual keying of the source documents was not a good alternative either, because of its labor-intensive nature. It was anticipated that, as the publishers of primary journals started computerizing their editorial processes, a significant number of relevant scientific articles would be in suitable machine-readable form. (p. 184)

Unforeseen problems included:

> The author summaries that were required by the editors of the primary journals would tend to obviate the need for automatic ab-

stracting . . . the authors of the primary journals did not always write abstracts that met the strict editorial requirements of the abstracting service, but . . . in general, the author abstracts were good. (p. 184)

[T]he editorial staff . . . feared that their jobs might be eliminated. This caused consternation among the editors and a tendency to overcriticize the [computer] program results and question its benefits. (p. 184)

Zamora and Zamora (1990) conclude that although the technology that they and their fellow researchers developed had transfer applications in other natural-language editing tasks and had helped to improve the production of abstracts at the Chemical Abstracts Service, it did not get beyond the research stage because of the slow progress in solving problems in computational linguistics. Or, as stated in their chapter in the collection *Managing Artificial Intelligence and Expert Systems,*

The fact that there were limiting factors in the application of the automatic abstracting technology, such as the unavailability of input . . . and the reticence of the editorial staff to embrace the approach, made it hard to justify its implementation. The project results themselves indicated that unless there was a breakthrough in the handling of semantics, the accomplishments would never be completely satisfactory or equal to manually produced abstracts.

One can only ask whether anything would be different if the project were conducted today. The answer is probably *no.* Although today we have better parsing technology and we can handle semantics better, there have not been any breakthroughs that would have a significant impact on the results. One can conclude reluctantly from this and similar experiences that progress in linguistics will continue to proceed at a snail's pace. Our only hope is that all of these small, incremental improvements will eventually enable us to solve today's problems satisfactorily. (p. 185)

EDITING OR REVISING COMPUTATIONAL ABSTRACTS

Attempts to render a poem in another language fall into three categories:

(1) *Paraphrastic*: offering a free version of the original, with omissions and additions prompted by the exigencies of form, the conventions attributed to the consumer, and the translator's ignorance . . .

(2) *Lexical* (or constructional): rendering the basic meaning of words (and their order) . . .

(3) *Literal*: rendering, as closely as the associative and syntactical capacities of another language allow, the exact contextual meaning of the original . . . (Nabokov. In: Pushkin, 1981, pp. vii–viii)

Should the production of computational abstracts in large volume become feasible (if that is not already the case), there may be a need for further human editorial work to ensure that their quality is commensurate with that of human-produced abstracts. With that possibility in mind, suggestions follow that are stimulated by Nabokov's thoughts (In: Pushkin, 1981) on how humans produce low- to high-quality (paraphrastic, lexical, to literal) translations. The suggestions for editing and revising computational abstracts are illustrated by again using the two sample articles that were described in Parts II through IV of this book.

Nabokov's three ascending categories for rendering low- to high-quality translations of poetry are redefined here into categories for the rendering of low- to high-quality computational abstracts.

Paraphrastic: Offering an unedited and unrevised abstract that is a computationally programmed version of the original natural-language text, with omissions prompted by the exigencies of form and content, conventions attributed to the user, and limitations of programs and computers in processing natural language. [This category of quality is roughly comparable to that for the unedited and unrevised version of the sample human-produced abstracts described in Part III, Responsive-to-Inventive Reading and Rules.]

Lexical (or constructional): Adding to whatever intrinsic values of unity and diversity are already within the paraphrastic abstract by human editing. [Comparable to the value-added editing of the sample abstracts described in Chapters 12 and 13.]

Literal: Approximating the exact contextual meaning of the original document being abstracted, indicatively or informatively, as closely as space limitations and the semantic and syntactical capacities of a human comparison of the lexical version of the computational abstract with the abstracted natural-language text allow. [Comparable to the meaning-making and further value-adding revising and editing of the sample abstracts, as described in Chapters 12 and 13.]

COMPUTATIONAL ABSTRACT FOR SAMPLE ARTICLE A

Sample Article A (a review of Forrester's book *Urban Dynamics*)—which was used to demonstrate human abstracting techniques in earlier chapters of this book—also had been abstracted, using a computer, as part of a dissertation research study by Mathis (1972). She used a test computational (automatic) abstracting system programmed for the IBM 370 computer. Called ADAM (Automatic Document Abstracting Method), the system was developed originally by Rush, Salvador, and Zamora (1971) at Ohio State University. Mathis introduced a modification to the ADAM system. She did not apply this modification to the computational abstract for Sample Article A shown below, but she did apply it to the computational abstract for Sample Article B, which will be discussed later in this chapter after the first abstract is given a prototypical edit and revision.

The first sample computational abstract comprises all of the sentences in 2 of the 15 paragraphs of the abstracted book review. Since the following version of that abstract (in the left-hand column) was not modified by the ADAM system that produced it, it will be considered a paraphrastic abstract, that is, one that has shortcomings, owing principally to the limitations of the program and the computer in processing natural language.

The shorter "lexical" version of this abstract, resulting from my editing using natural knowledge of grammar, usage, syntax, semantics, and style, is shown in the right-hand column.

Original—"paraphrastic" version

Forrester, a professor at M.I.T.'s Sloan School of Management, relies on a computer model he developed to simulate the growth, decline, and stagnation of a hypothetical city (or "urban area") from birth to old age (250 years). Such methods have a great deal of potential for the analysis of urban problems and have al-

Edited—"lexical" version

Forrester relies on his computer model to simulate the growth, decline, and stagnation of a hypothetical city from birth to old age (250 years). Such methods have great potential for analyzing urban problems, having shown value in specific limited applications. Development of truly useful and trustworthy urban

ready demonstrated their value in a number of specific, though limited applications. However, the development of truly useful and trustworthy urban simulation models remains a distant objective and will require much greater resources than have yet been devoted to the task. Before adequate models become available, many inadequate ones will be put forward. Forrester's model is a conspicuous example. In his first chapter Forrester warns the reader that caution should be exercised in applying the model to actual situations. Subsequently, however, he expresses few reservations about the model's validity and freely uses it as a basis for prescribing public policy. The influence of tax rates on employment and population structure in Forrester's city is powerful and pervasive. "Managerial-professional" and "labor" families are assumed to be repelled by high tax rates, whereas the "underemployed" are indifferent to them. High tax rates, moreover, discourage the formation of new enterprises and accelerate the aging of existing ones. There are still other adverse effects: high taxes retard construction of both premium and worker housing, which in turn discourages the kinds of people who live in these kinds of housing from moving into the city or remaining there.

models, however, remains distant and will require much greater resources than have yet been applied. Before adequate models become available, many inadequate ones will be put forward, such as Forrester's. Initially, he warns that caution should be exercised in actually applying the model. Later, however, he expresses few reservations about its validity and freely uses it in prescribing public policy. The influence of tax rates on employment and population structure in Forrester's city is powerful and pervasive. "Managerial-professional" and "labor" families are assumed to be repelled by high taxes, but the underemployed are indifferent to them. High taxes discourage the formation of new enterprises and accelerate the aging of existing ones. Also, they retard construction of both premium and worker housing, which in turn discourages the residents of such housing from moving into the city or remaining there.

For the third or "literal" version of this computational abstract, I attempted to add more value to, and make more meaningful, the lexical version of the abstract by reviewing it against the edited and revised abstract of this book review, displayed earlier on page 90. (If I hadn't already completed this process, I would have reviewed the lexical version of the computational abstract directly against the full 15 paragraphs of the abstracted book review.) As a result of this review, I suggest adding the two indicative sentences that begin the abstract on page 90 to this computational abstract to show more clearly the purpose or "aboutness" of the book review and the topics that are discussed within it. Also, to make this abstract more meaningful, I suggest adding the penultimate informative sentence from the abstract on page 90. These three additional sentences are italicized in the literal version of the computational abstract for Sample Article A that follows.

Edited—"literal" version

The use of systems-analysis techniques and computer modeling as proposed in Jay W. Forrester's Urban Dynamics is evaluated. The interrelationships of public policy and financing, taxes, municipal expenditures, employment, housing, population mobility, and land supply and use are considered. Forrester relies on his computer model to simulate the growth, decline, and stagnation of a hypothetical city from birth to old age (250 years). Such methods have great potential for analyzing urban problems, having shown value in specific limited applications. Development of truly useful and trustworthy urban models, however, remains distant and will require much greater resources than have yet been applied. Before adequate models become available, many inadequate ones will be put forward, such as Forrester's. Initially, he warns that caution should be exercised in actually applying the model. Later, however, he expresses few reservations about its validity and freely uses it in prescribing public policy. The influence of tax rates on employment and population structure in Forrester's city is powerful and pervasive. "Managerial-professional" and "labor" families are assumed to be repelled by high taxes, but the underemployed are indifferent to them. High taxes discourage the formation of new enterprises and accelerate the aging of existing ones. Also, they retard construction of both premium and worker housing, which in turn discourages the residents of such housing from moving into the city or remaining there. *The reviewer recommends that funding from nonlocal sources should be used to reduce municipal taxes rather than to increase municipal expenditures.*

COMPUTATIONAL ABSTRACT FOR SAMPLE ARTICLE B

The first version of Computational Abstract B is a lexical one, because the initial or paraphrastic version that was produced using a computer was also modified in the computer. As mentioned earlier, Sample Abstract B was written for the article "Addition of Oxygen Atoms to Olefins at Low Temperature. IV. Rearrangements."

Two versions of the lexical abstract will be displayed below: (a) Mathis's (1972) "improved computer-produced abstract," which totals 364 words (four words less than the 368 in the paraphrastic abstract; the four deleted words in the improved version are shown in boldface type); and (b) my further editing of version (a), which contains 338 words. (Although it was originally printed out in all capital letters, without italics, the computer-produced version of the abstract is shown here in initial caps and italics, where appropriate.)

(a) **Computational Abstract B, Lexical** (slightly edited, using the ADAM system)

> A consideration of the oxygen atom addition to *cis*- and *trans*-2-butene in the temperature region 77 to 113 K led to the formulation of a new transition intermediate. In this intermediate, the oxygen atom is represented as bound in a loose, three-membered ring with, and in the plane of, the olefinic structure of the reactant. Observations on 2-butenes have been extended to several more straight-chain, internal olefins in the low-temperature region. Comparison of the *trans*-epoxide to ketone ratios from the *cis*- vs the *trans*-olefin with increasing size of the olefin indicates that these ratios diverge. **The second is that** reaction of oxygen atoms in the low-temperature region tends to be more stereospecific with *trans*- than with *cis*-olefins. Carbonyl compounds constitute a sizable fraction of the products of the oxygen atom addition to olefins in the low-temperature region, and, as has been noted, an intramolecular group migration is required for carbonyl formation. The principal carbonyl product in the *trans*-2-butene reaction at 90 K is 2-butanone. The formation of this ketone requires the migration of H. Compared to the migration of the methyl group, that of H is slightly favored. *cis*-2-butene is not useful for the comparison, as both of the hydrogen atoms attached to the olefinic carbon pair are suppressed through interaction with oxygen in the complex. The relative quantities of 2-butanone to isobutyraldehyde is taken as a measure of the ratio of migration of

the hydrogen atom to the methyl group. Reactions were effected at 90 K in the apparatus routinely used for the purpose. The olefins were diluted 10 to 1 with propane. The exposure time of oxygen atoms was 5 minutes, and about 1% of the olefin was reacted. The products were determined at 135 and a helium flow of 100 cc/ minute. The *cis* and *trans* isomers of 3,4-epoxy-3,4-dimethyl-hexane were not separable. Localization of the oxygen atom in the transition complex *preceding* alkyl group rearrangement is not in accord with the experimental results. At 90 K, the ratio of addition to C-2 is 1.6 times that to C-3. For MEP, addition of the oxygen atom to that carbon atom of the double bond to which the two methyl groups are attached would be expected to be favored.

(b) **Computational Abstract B, Lexical** (moderately edited, by a human editor)

(1)*   Consideration of O atom addition to *cis*- and *trans*-2-butene at temperatures between 77 to 113 K led to formulation of a new transition intermediate, in which the O atom is represented as bound in a loose, three-membered ring with, and in the plane of,

(2)   the olefinic structure of the reactant. Observations on 2-butenes were extended to other straight-chain, internal olefins at low tem-

(3)   peratures. Comparison of *trans*-epoxide to ketone ratios from the *cis*- vs the *trans*-olefin with increasing size of the olefin indicates

(4)   that these ratios diverge. Reaction of O atoms at low temperature tends to be more stereospecific with *trans*- than with *cis*-olefins.

(5)   Carbonyl compounds constitute a sizable fraction of the products of the O atom addition to olefins at low temperature, and an intramolecular group migration is required for carbonyl forma-

(6)   tion. The principal carbonyl product in the *trans*-2-butene reaction at 90 K is 2-butanone, formation of which requires the mi-

(7)   gration of H. Compared to the migration of the methyl group,

(8)   that of H is slightly favored. *cis*-2-butene is not useful for the comparison, as both of the H atoms attached to the olefinic carbon pair are suppressed through interaction with O in the com-

(9)   plex. The relative quantities of 2-butanone to isobutyraldehyde are taken as a measure of the ratio of migration of the H atom to

(10)   the methyl group. Reactions were effected at 90 K in a standard

(11)   apparatus. The olefins were diluted 10 to 1 with propane.

(12)   The exposure time of O atoms was 5 minutes, and about 1% of

---

*Sentence number

(13)   the olefin was reacted. The products were determined at 135° and
(14)   a helium flow of 100 cc/minute. The *cis* and *trans* isomers of 3,4-
(15)   epoxy-3,4-dimethylhexane were not separable. Localization of the
       O atom in the transition complex preceding alkyl group rear-
(16)   rangement is not in accord with the experimental results. At 90
(17)   K, the ratio of addition to C-2 is 1.6 times that to C-3. For MEP,
       addition of the O atom to that C atom of the double bond to
       which the two methyl groups are attached would probably be fa-
       vored.

The initial paraphrastic version of the computer-generated computational abstract for Sample Article B has thus been transformed into
a lexical version by editing it internally to add to its intrinsic value.
Now it will be further transformed into a literal abstract to add more
quality to and make more meaning in it. This will be done by revising
it, by comparing it against the full text of the printed version of the article from which it was abstracted, including the author's abstract. This
process will comprise the rejection or addition of sentences.

Rejection of sentences. For the literal version of the abstract, the first
edited sentence was rejected because it contained background information from earlier research. Seven more sentences (7 through 9 and 11
through 14) were rejected to achieve a more uniform balance in the in-
formational elements. Also, sentence 10 was moved to become sentence
2 so that the abstract would more closely resemble a standard informative abstract.

Addition of sentences. An author abstract containing five sentences
was included in the published version of the article from which Computational Abstract B was created. To add more meaning, the last three of
these sentences will be added at the end of the revised computational abstract. The resulting literal version, less the rejected sentences and with
the added author's sentences (underlined), reads as follows:

(c) **Computational Abstract B, Literal** (revised by an editor)

    Observations on 2-butenes were extended to other straight-chain,
    internal olefins at low temperatures. Reactions were effected at 90

K in a standard apparatus. Comparison of *trans*-epoxide to ketone ratios from the *cis-* vs the *trans*-olefin with increasing size of the olefin indicates that these ratios diverge. Reaction of O atoms at low temperature tends to be more stereospecific with *trans-* than with *cis*-olefins. Carbonyl compounds constitute a sizable fraction of the products of the O atom addition to olefins at low temperature, and an intramolecular group migration is required for carbonyl formation. The principal carbonyl product in the *trans*-2-butene reaction at 90 K is 2-butanone, formation of which requires the migration of H. Localization of the O atom in the transition complex preceding alkyl group rearrangement is not in accord with the experimental results. At 90 K, the ratio of addition to C-2 is 1.6 times that to C-3. For MEP (3-ethyl-2-methyl-2-pentene), addition of the O atom to that C atom of the double bond to which the two methyl groups are attached would probably be favored. <u>Rearrangements involving migration of alkyl groups and localization of O on one of the carbon atoms of the olefinic pair occur in a concerted manner. This was shown from the reactions of MEP and two of its isomers. Clearly, independent rates cannot be associated with migrating alkyl groups, and additional factors, other than electron density, determined the position of addition of the O atom.</u>

Although they have been applied to the products of a system that was in the developmental stage, the editing and revising of these sample computational abstracts demonstrate some of the procedures that might be used in post-editing computational abstracts or other summary-like computational information processing representations. As noted, these procedures are rooted in human knowledge of grammar, usage, syntax, semantics, and style as they apply to reading, writing, editing, and revising.

CHAPTER 17

Documental Information Processing and the Thought Processes

Synopsis of Categories

Class Fourteen
The Mind and Ideas[1]

930 THOUGHT

<exercise of the intellect>

NOUNS **1 thought, thinking, cogitation,** cerebration, ideation, noesis, mentation, intellection, intellectualization, ratiocination; using one's head *or* noodle <nonformal>; workings of the mind; **reasoning** 934; **brainwork, headwork,** mental labor *or* effort, mental act *or* process, act of thought, mental *or* intellectual exercise; deep-think <nonformal>; **way of thinking,** habit of thought *or* mind, thought-pattern; heavy thinking, straight thinking; conception, conceit <old>, conceptualization; abstract thought, imageless thought; excogitation, thinking out *or* through; thinking aloud; **idea** 931; creative thought 985.2

2 consideration, contemplation, reflection, speculation, meditation, musing, rumination, deliberation, lucubration, brooding, study, **pondering,** weighing, revolving, turning over in the mind, looking at from all angles, noodling *or* noodling around <nonformal>; lateral thought *or* thinking; advisement, counsel

932 ABSENCE OF THOUGHT

NOUNS **1 thoughtlessness,** thoughtfreeness; **vacuity.** vacancy, **emptiness of mind, empty-headedness,** blankness, mental blankness, blankmindedness; fatuity, inanity, foolishness 922; tranquillity, calm of mind; **nirvana,** ataraxia, calm *or* tranquillity of mind; **oblivion,** forgetfulness, lack *or* loss of memory, amnesia; quietism, passivity, apathy; blank mind, fallow mind, tabula rasa; unintelligence 921

VERBS **2 not think, make the mind a blank,** let the mind lie fallow; **not think of,** not consider, be unmindful of; **not enter one's mind** *or* **head,** be far from one's mind *or* head *or* thoughts; pay no attention *or* mind

3 get it off one's mind, get it off one's chest <nonformal>, clear the mind, relieve one's mind; **put it out of one's thoughts,** dismiss from the mind *or* thoughts, push from one's thoughts, put away thought

—Roget's International Thesaurus, 5th ed.
(Robert L. Chapman, ed., 1992, pp. 645, 647)

As Donald F. Kent (In: Chapman, 1992), a physician (as was Roget), recounts in his brief biography of Peter Mark Roget in the fifth edition of *Roget's International Thesaurus*, besides Roget's work in medicine and science, one of the many other ways that he exercised his intellect was as a lexicographer. (I include lexicographers or classifiers within the ranks of documental information processors.)

Kent notes that Roget "dwelt in a world of language and his orderly, systematic mind lent itself to classification. More than a list of synonyms, more than a dictionary, the thesaurus Roget devised and constantly improved upon during this time was a unique ordering of the English language to be used by those desiring to impart an exacting felicitous tone to written or spoken material." (p. x)

One hundred and forty years after the publication of the first edition of Roget's original *Thesaurus of English Words and Phrases, Classified and Arranged so as to Facilitate the Expression of Ideas and Assist in Literary Composition*, Chapman (1992), a retired professor of English and a practicing lexicographer, has edited the fifth edition of *Roget's International Thesaurus*. One of the many features that Chapman has introduced to add more value and meaning to the fifth edition is a "Synopsis of Categories" that shapes his "developmental-existential" scheme for this edition. Dr. Chapman explains that "The notion has been to make the arrangement analogous with the development of the human individual and the human race. It is more associational and durational than logical. This seems to me 'the simplest and most natural' array in the mind of our own time." (p. xvii)

The "Synopsis of Categories" contains 1,073 categories subsumed under 15 classes. Class Fourteen (The Mind and Ideas), from which partial extracts for two categories (930 Thought and 932 Absence of Thought) are shown at the beginning of this chapter, contains the largest number of categories: 255.

This fifth edition of *Roget's International Thesaurus* is an invaluable thought-evoking, eliciting, prompting, summoning, and inducing English-language guide for all human information processors, particularly such documental information processors as lexicographers, classifiers, indexers, abstractors, and translators.

INDEXING/CLASSIFYING AND THE THOUGHT (COGNITIVE) PROCESSES

> Information science is a cognitive science, that is, it deals with thought processes, one of the most difficult areas to investigate. . . . It becomes obvious that the more we study the two cognitive ends of the picture, that is, the cognitive processes which produce information, and the cognitive processes which occur on the receipt of information, the more we may be able to improve and control the processes of information storage and retrieval to attain desired results. (Farradane, 1980a, p. 75)

In his writings, Farradane (1955, 1967, 1976, 1979, 1980a,b,c) discussed both the associational and discriminatory relationships between thought, truth, language, cognitive processes, knowledge, meaning, information, information science, information retrieval, communication theory, and the documental information processing functions of indexing in particular and classification in general.

Farradane's (1979) studies on relational indexing were "an attempt to simulate the structure of knowledge, or mental relations between concepts, and some of the rules relating to the transformations possible in that structure. . . in order to apply them to indexing information reproducibly in forms that will be suitable for any human user." (p. 76)

Just a few examples of the many associational and discriminatory relationships that Farradane conceptualized in developing his theories on the scope of information science and the practice of relational indexing are:

> 1. Knowledge is a memorable record of a process in the brain, something available only in the mind. Information is defined as a physical surrogate of knowledge (e.g., language) used for communication. (1980c, p. 77)

> 2. Relational indexing . . . is a means of expressing relations on a basis of the mechanisms of thought, to be converted directly into indexing notation. . . . [It] tends to indicate the types of words needed for adequate expression of meaning, and obviates the need for casually used compound terms. (1980a, p. 268)

3. Since the true basis of meaning exists in our thought, the system of relations [in relational indexing] is based upon an analysis of thought processes, as investigated in the psychology of thinking. (1980a, p. 268)

4. [The thought processes] are basically much simpler than might have been supposed, and yield a system comprising a limited number (9) of categories of relations between concepts. [The nine categories are concurrence, equivalence, distinctness, self-activity, dimensional, action, association, appurtenance, and functional dependence (causation).] (1980a, p. 268)

Farradane (1980c) found from considerable experience of relational indexing "that the method induces a considerable degree of intuitive control of indexing to produce accuracy of interpretation of the meaning of a subject . . . with relatively short training (one month) of intelligent people, consistent indexing can be achieved. Some degree of subject knowledge is desirable." (p. 323)

Beghtol (1986) has examined the learning and cognitive processes that operate when a human bibliographically classifies a document. The documental classifying process is a secondary one that "mediates between recognition of the primary aboutness of the document-to-be-classified and the tertiary expression of its aboutness in a named class by means of its corresponding notation in a particular bibliographic classification system." (p. 100) Meaning in a document is the reason a user may want to retrieve it.

Beghtol holds that a theory of the cognitive process of classifying documents must explain how the classifier sequentially:

1. [T]ransforms the surface structure of the document into its deep propositional structure;

2. [T]ransforms the surface structure of the classification system into its deep propositional logical structure;

3. [J]oins these two deep propositional structures using the actual system of the classification schedules and instructions as an artificially-constructed virtual system for expressing the natural language actual systems of primary documents; and

4. [T]ransforms the resulting single propositional structure of "classification system applied to document" back into the surface structure of the classification schedules, generates the apposite notation, and concludes that the document has been appropriately

placed in the class with other documents to which it is most
nearly intellectually and intertextually similar. (pp. 102–103)

Extracting from the abstract in Farrow's (1991) article, "A Cognitive
Process Model of Document Indexing," we learn that task descriptions
for a model of text comprehension by indexers (as well as classifiers and
abstractors) indicate that the comprehension process differs from normal
fluent reading in respect to operational time constraints, which lead to
text being scanned rapidly for perceptual cues to aid gist comprehension,
because comprehension is task-oriented rather than learning-oriented.
Also, this process is immediately followed by the production of an abstract, index, or classification.

Farrow agrees with Mitchell (1982), Just and Carpenter (1987), and
Smith (1988) that the reader's comprehension of text involves "top-
down" and "bottom-up" processing. The former "uses information that
is not contained in the text, but is part of the world-knowledge that the
author possesses and which he assumes that his readers will also possess. This kind of processing is termed conceptual, to distinguish it
from the perceptual or bottom-up processing of the information that is
actually contained in the text." (p. 151)

Farrow's cognitive process model of document indexing highlights the
importance of conceptual processing and the "consequent need for indexers to be familiar with the subject matter of the texts they are working
with; the limited comprehension obtainable by scanning and the types of
perceptual cues in scanning text and their use; and the nature and importance of expertise in the performance of a professional task." (p. 163)
For the education and training of indexers, the model is helpful in pin-
pointing the causes of inadequate or inaccurate indexing.

ABSTRACTING AND THE THOUGHT PROCESSES

As one of the assignments in my course, my students had to write
an abstract of a published paper. The paper itself was brief,
simple, and well written. I was dismayed to find that at least half
of my students misread the paper in three major ways. First, they
referred to 20-day-old rats, although the age of the animals was
never given—the article described 20-gram rats; second, they
talked about specific activity of the cholesterol injected, whereas
the specific activity was never stated—the figure they had got hold

of was actually the number of millicuries injected per kilogram of rat body weight, and they had misread it as mc/mg; last, and most amazing of all, they gave conclusions directly opposite to those indicated both by the data and by the authors of the article they were abstracting! (Woodford, 1967, p. 744)

In his article, "Sounder Thinking Through Clearer Writing," Woodford (1967) discusses the causes and effects of the inferior writing that is published in some scientific journals. This writing often results from "an inward confusion of thought." (p. 745) Exposure to it "exerts a corrupting influence on young scientists—on their writing, their reading, and their thinking." (p. 744)

Woodford recommends that students complete a graduate course in scientific writing to strengthen their scientific thinking. The course should concentrate on "logic, precision, and clarity; on how these qualities can be achieved in writing; and on how such achievemment strengthens the corresponding faculties in thinking." (p. 745)

Specifically for abstractors, for sounder thinking while writing clearer abstracts, I suggest:

1. A logical format for composing the abstract, preferably purpose- or findings-oriented, should be selected, and the required order for representing the relevant information should be adhered to.

2. A judgment on what information is relevant for inclusion in the abstract should be suspended until the full text has been scanned.

3. Multiple versions of the same relevant information in a text should be compared, and the most pertinent details from the individual versions should be consolidated for extraction into the abstract.

4. Authors of abstracts should assign precise meanings to the words that they use in their abstracts. Documental information processing abstractors should attempt to substitute more precise words for any unclear or ambiguous ones that they extract from the material being abstracted. The substitutions, however, should be made *only* after the abstractors are convinced that there is not the slightest possibility that the author's meaning will be distorted in the process.

5. The significance of certain relevant information should not be overly emphasized at the expense of other equally or more relevant information through careless or inadequate reading of the text of the basic document.

6. Abstracts should be composed in such a way that no doubt is created in the reader's mind as to whether the results, conclusions, and recommendations presented therein are, in fact, the author's, rather than those of other researchers whose work the author has cited in the basic document.

7. All abstractors should persistently motivate themselves to use clear and sound thinking whether they are writing single abstracts as authors or large volumes of abstracts as documental information processing abstractors.

Through these and other ways of exercising the thought processes while abstracting, not only will well-structured and meaningful abstracts be written, but the abstractors themselves will improve their comprehension and gain additional practical conceptual knowledge in such subjects as semantics, syntax, grammar, usage, reading, writing, editing, and revising.

PART VI

PROFESSIONAL
RELATIONSHIPS

INDICATIVE ABSTRACT

Cooperative professional relationships between managers, abstractors, and other documental information processors are discussed. Quality control functions of users, sponsors, and managers of abstracting services are considered. Responsibilities of editors or reviewers of abstracts are described, including those of effectively communicating with, training, and evaluating abstractors, and improving the style and content of original English-language and translation abstracts. The topics of abstracting as a profession and the professional status of documental information processing abstractors are examined.

CHAPTER 18

Cooperative not Copyright Management of Abstracting and Abstractors

With this notice, management at Chemical Abstracts Service is using the copyright function as it was intended—to control access to their products and services. Most information system managers do restrict their use of the copyright function to its intended purpose. These are potentially "cooperative" managers. Cooperative managers know that the policies and procedures for producing their information products are not static, figuratively copyrightable ones, subject only to rare adjustments, but are, in fact, dynamic ones requiring their constant attention, monitoring, and adjustment.

PRODUCT AWARENESS AND QUALITY CONTROL

In abstracting, product awareness is knowing what an acceptable abstract is, what actions are appropriate to minimize the publication and distribution of unacceptable abstracts, and when these actions should be

145

taken. Product awareness and quality control should be concerns of everyone involved in the abstracting process—from users at the top to sponsors and managers of abstracting services, editors or reviewers, and abstractors at the source.

Users who identify inferior published abstracts should inform sponsors or managers of abstracting services so that they can take steps to improve the quality of the abstracts. Sponsors who contract for abstracting services should familiarize themselves thoroughly with the fundamentals of abstracting and the value and limitations of abstracts. They should specify precisely their preference for the type, structure, style, and content of the abstracts; monitor the quality of the abstracts that they receive; and promptly inform managers of abstracting services about significant shortcomings in their abstracts or lapses in procedures. Managers of abstracting services should make routine quality control checks of abstracts and discuss with the editorial staff any problems that are identified. Editors, reviewers, and abstractors should seek to identify and correct as many shortcomings as possible during the actual abstract preparation process.

SELECTING AND EVALUATING ABSTRACTORS

Undergraduate or graduate degree? Scientist or nonscientist? Specialist or generalist? Linguist or nonlinguist? Indexer or nonindexer? Librarian or nonlibrarian? Who should be hired and trained to write documental information processing abstracts on scientific, technical, or scholarly subjects? Given the choice, most managers would, of course, prefer the better trained or more experienced candidates. But the higher the qualifications and the fewer the candidates, the greater the gap may be between salary requirements and available funds, and the lower the potential will be for retaining these individuals after they are trained. Managers, therefore, often are obliged to hire and train individuals with fewer qualifications than they might prefer. Whether highly or moderately qualified, once an information processing abstractor candidate is provisionally hired, it is imperative that his or her potential to write quality abstracts productively be determined promptly.

The manager therefore must evaluate new abstractors by using a set of performance criteria. In Chapter 15 of their monograph *Abstracting Scientific and Technical Literature: an Introductory Guide and Text for*

Scientists, Abstractors, and Management, Maizell, Smith, and Singer (1971) list 12 such criteria. These include factors such as promptness, accuracy, clarity, readability, completeness, and selectivity. With the assistance of editors or reviewers, managers should be able to determine quickly how well a provisional abstractor can meet these and other performance criteria.

After introductory training in the fundamentals of abstracting, the abstractor should be assigned three to five papers or monographs containing diverse subject matter for original abstracting. These materials should *not* contain author abstracts. If author abstracts have been published with the materials, they should be deleted on the copy that will be used by the trainees. After they are abstracted, the abstracts should be carefully edited by an editor, reviewer, or senior abstractor. The supervisor should discuss the results with the trainee, emphasizing points on structure, style, unity, and conciseness.

A second batch of twice as many materials should then be assigned for original abstracting, with the possible inclusion of items from the first group that require extensive rewriting. After the resulting abstracts are edited, the manager should have a clear idea of how long it will take the provisional abstractor to become proficient.

PROFESSIONAL RELATIONSHIPS AMONG DOCUMENTAL INFORMATION SPECIALISTS

Information specialists, including processors such as catalogers, abstractors, indexers, and translators, information retrieval search analysts, bibliographic lexicographers, editors, and other abstract journal or information acquisition, processing, storage, and retrieval system production workers, have opportunities to maintain a community of professional relationships. Abstractors for some information systems expand their professional relationships through additional processing work as indexers, translators, editors, or contributors to the production control of abstract journals.

CHAPTER 19

Notes to Editors of Abstracts

This article is worthless!

—ABSTRACTOR'S NOTE TO EDITOR

But you wrote a good abstract nevertheless!

—EDITOR'S RETURN NOTE

In addition to self-editing by abstractors, almost all abstracts receive further editing, revising, or reviewing before they are published, filed manually, or stored in computers or on compact disks. The editing or reviewing ranges from a minimal amount for camera-ready abstracts, to a moderate amount for most conventional informative and indicative abstracts, to a very thorough pre- and post-publication review for some lengthy and highly detailed digest-like abstracts of long or complex primary documents.

Editors of abstracts may hold a variety of titles, including the general one of editor or reviewer to that of managing editor, with such intermediary titles as associate or assistant editor. For quality control, these editors may orally discuss abstracts and abstracting or exchange notes or memoranda with sponsors, managers, and voluntary, free-lance, or staff abstractors. These discussions or notes could cover such topics as abstracting procedures, style, and content; deadlines; individual abstractor performance; and training.

SUGGESTED READING RULES FOR EDITORS

The five suggested interrogatory rules for self-editing of abstracts via connective reading (Chapter 12) also apply when additional editing is done by editors or reviewers.

Rule 1. Is the abstract properly structured and unified?

Rule 2. Is the content of the abstract coherent and concise?

Rule 3. After scanning the text of the document being abstracted, is it clear that the fullest amount of meaning feasible has been represented in the draft abstract?

Rule 4. Does this abstract conform fully with standard abstracting guidelines or those of the sponsoring abstracting service, journal publisher, or data base vendor?

Rule 5. Are there any other problems with the style or content of the draft abstract that might be resolved expediently by consulting with other abstractors, editors, technical reviewers, or subject experts, as available and appropriate?

For abstracts that contain major shortcomings, editors must decide whether they routinely will edit the inferior abstract and, in the process, spend more than the standard amount of time alloted for editing, or return the abstract to the abstractor for revision. Whenever it is feasible, the latter step is recommended, because it is the abstractor's responsibility to produce acceptable abstracts. The quality of his or her subsequent abstracts should improve thereby, and the editor's productive time and ability to improve other abstracts are enhanced. Time permitting, editors should attempt to point out all major shortcomings and recurring minor ones to abstractors by arranging for the shortcomings to be marked on edited copy and returned to the abstractor, as well as through periodic reviews with the abstractor.

EDITORIAL FEEDBACK

The development and maintenance of good-quality abstracting services require routine, open, two-way communication between editors and abstractors. Whether splitting hairs over split infinitives, explaining the reasons for preferring either purpose- or results-oriented abstracts, or pointing out the major flaws in style and content that require the rewriting of an abstract, editors should always be tactful and instructive. Each criticism worthy of being brought to an abstractor's attention should be accompanied by constructive advice for improvement or reference to written instructions. Oral or written communications with abstractors should be timely and accurate. Editors also can profit when there is a two-way flow of information on correct abstracting procedures. In addition to verbal communication, the use of notes or memoranda is beneficial. Abstractors also can use standard forms from editors to abstractors, similar to the one shown in Figure 7, to forward their comments and questions on procedures and style to editors.

Style Points and Reminders for Abstractors
(These style points or reminders result from the editing process and are forwarded to assist in maintaining a high degree of clarity, coherence, and conciseness in your abstracts.)
Abstracting (General):
Abstracts (Specific) Purpose: Methodology: Results–Conclusions–Recommendations: Other:
Abstractor _____ Date _____ Editor(s) _____

FIGURE 7   Sample form for style points and reminders.

EDITORS AS INSTRUCTORS

Editors must be knowledgeable enough to introduce background materials on abstracting in a clear, comprehensive, and stimulating way. They must evaluate accurately the performance of abstractors during training and their progress after they become qualified. Moreover, editors must be capable of identifying the shortcomings of individuals who fail to respond to instructions within a reasonable period of time. This information should be recorded in abstractor trainee evaluations to assist managers in deciding whether it will be counterproductive, both to the trainee and to the abstracting service, if he or she is retained.

TRANSLATIONS AND TRANSLATORS

Abstracts written by those for whom English is a second language or abstracts written from poorly translated materials often serve as a difficult, but rewarding, challenge to the editor's critical reading skills. Communication with translators whose fluency in English is only fair often is an equally difficult challenge to the editor's skills as an instructor. In addition to resolving standard editing and training problems, editors in either situation also must remove the remaining language barriers that were not overcome during the translation process.

Editors should be particularly alert for the following flaws in translated abstracts: nonstandard word choice (e.g., falling hair, poisoning, and radar impulses for alopecia, treatment, and radar pulses in abstracts of medical, toxicological, and communications research papers, respectively); ambiguity; lack of conciseness; awkward sentence structure; and faults in parallelism, pluralization, and the use of articles and prepositions.

CHAPTER 20

Abstracting as a Profession

905 Help Wanted
ABSTRACTOR International health publication. Familiarity with health sciences and college degree required. Foreign language preferred. Convenient location. Full time. Call 999-0000, ext. 2460. EOE

Individuals find abstracting assignments through referrals by persons involved in or familiar with information systems and publications, or in response to advertisements similar to the one shown above. In this chapter, subjective comments on the benefits and consequences of abstracting are presented, along with more objective information on how to enter the field and professional training programs.

ASSESSMENT OF ABSTRACTING IMPACTS

The environmental impact statements that I once abstracted for the journal *EIS: Key to Environmental Impact Statements* were often lengthy, and so were some of the early abstracts that were published. Part of the lengthiness of the abstracts resulted from attempts to summarize impartially the primary positive and negative environmental impacts of each

153

project or program for which a statement had been published and circulated for public review. That training in impartial reporting has influenced the preparation of the following summary of a few of the pros and cons of choosing abstracting as an occupation.

Positive Impacts of Abstracting

Within documental information processing systems, abstracts are one of the most fundamental and significant writing forms. Abstracting is an excellent training experience for writing in other, more challenging forms, including content analyses, state-of-the-art literature reviews, and technical proposals.

Abstractors influence the decision-making processes of indexers, researchers, and other writers, and contribute to their effectiveness as a function of the quality of the abstracts that they produce. With each new document that is accepted for abstracting, the abstractor is given an opportunity to master its information content, to maintain high standards in quality, and to gain the satisfaction that comes from meeting deadlines.

Abstractors who are required to extract and record bibliographic information or to index the materials that they abstract can broaden the range and market value of their information processing skills. Abstractors who are furnished with constructive evaluations from editors, reviewers, managers, or readers of their abstracts either receive recognition for well-written abstracts or are given opportunities to improve their reading, writing, and self-editing skills when shortcomings in their abstracts are brought to their attention.

Abstractors with translating skills can improve their language proficiency and technical writing skills, in both familiar and unfamiliar subject areas, when requested to write abstracts because of a shortage of qualified translators. Translators also may derive satisfaction from the knowledge that they are contributing to worldwide dissemination of scientific and technical findings and scholarly thought. The quality of their translations may be a deciding factor in determining whether additional resources will be invested in preparing full-text translations for the documents that they abstract.

Abstracting serves as a daily, on-the-job, continuing educational experience, primarily in analytical reading and secondarily in thinking, writing, editing, and revising.

Negative Impacts of Abstracting

As was usually true with the projects and programs that were described in the environmental impact statements that I abstracted, many of the positive aspects of working as an abstractor can be counterbalanced with approximately reciprocal negative ones.

Writing concise, condensed versions of scientific, technical, and scholarly papers is difficult and requires mental energy, sustained concentration, and self-discipline. Full-time abstractors quickly become aware of this. Some students who attempt to fit an abstracting job into their academic schedules to help with their education costs, have found that, although the work is not as physically demanding as other part-time jobs that are available to them, abstracting unduly drains the supply of mental energy that they have budgeted for their studies.

Although less so than indexing and cataloging, abstracting is a low-profile profession. Certain abstract journals will give credit to abstractors by inserting their names on the masthead or in parentheses at the end of their abstracts. More in keeping with their task of condensing information, some abstractors are identified only by their intitials when their abstracts are published. But the majority of professional abstractors receive recognition of their names or initials only from their editors, not from the readers of their abstracts.

Abstractors are sometimes expected to complete both sides of an information data sheet; that is, besides writing the abstract for an article or book, they also may be asked to prepare an index or to extract and record the cataloging information from the primary document, usually in accordance with lengthy, precise instructions. The compensation for such extra work is often less than commensurate with the time and effort that are expended in doing it.

The quality of abstracts may be criticized by editors, reviewers, indexers, information retrieval analysts, supervisors, managers, and the users of the information service. Or, at the opposite extreme, and to the detriment of the abstractor's skills, he or she may work for a service that overemphasizes the need for the timely submission and publication of abstracts while showing only superficial concern for their style and content by minimizing or bypassing the editing and review processes altogether.

When the skills of abstractor and translator are combined, abstractors may at times be expected to demonstrate the expertise of simultaneous translators or interpreters at the United Nations, but at far lower pay.

Whether linguists or not, abstractors who are occasionally obliged to edit the abstract of, or to abstract, a poorly translated paper for which the original text in the foreign language is not available must use the highest editing or abstracting skills, combined with a touch of linguistic guesswork, to prepare an acceptable abstract.

The majority of documents that are acquired by other information specialists for processing by catalogers, abstractors, and indexers possess enough lasting value to justify recording and storage in information retrieval systems. But some papers that are assigned for abstracting and indexing have a content value that is so low that, rather than being abstracted, they should have been stored permanently only between the covers of the primary publications that they appeared in. Once assigned for processing, however, they should be routinely abstracted and indexed following standard processing procedures.

Finally, human documental information processing abstractors are threatened, although not seriously as yet, with partial or full replacement by computational information processing systems. Researchers, with this goal in mind, are writing and testing innumerable algorithms with the aim of instructing machines to "read" text and "write" abstracts electronically.

These, then, are some of the benefits and consequences of writing abstracts. On balance, I consider the work to be challenging and educational, with good potential for advancement to more demanding analytical and managerial assignments. But each person who is contemplating becoming an abstractor should carefully assess both the consequences and the benefits before deciding to enter the field.

TURNING PROFESSIONAL

Graduates of library or information science programs are among the most likely candidates to become professional abstractors. Many have completed survey or practical courses on the subject, and some have gained practical experience as free-lance abstractors. A few librarians occasionally write abstracts for public, governmental, or special library collections; but most of the librarians of my acquaintance indicate that they prefer to pursue careers within other library or information science fields. These include reference or information retrieval work, collection development, programming, indexing, and cataloging. Many of those who do write abstracts do so only on an interim basis.

A more fruitful and diverse source of professional abstractors for secondary publications and information systems is that comprising university graduates from academic programs other than library or information science, or individuals crossing over to the information science field from careers other than library science. Abstractors in this group initially tend to be subject specialists rather than generalists. But after gaining practical experience in abstracting, many perform as both specialists and generalists. These abstractor candidates include recent graduates who have been unable to find challenging work in their chosen fields of study, retirees from other professions seeking second careers, and free-lancers who write abstracts to supplement their incomes. A third and smaller group of abstractor candidates for information services is provided by transfers from within the staff of these systems. Data clerks, document acquisition specialists, catalogers, indexers, and information retrieval analysts are among the specialists who are potentially eligible for cross-training as abstractors.

PROFESSIONAL TRAINING

The training of professional abstractors is conducted in four general locations: on-site at information processing centers, in the home or other appropriate premises by self-instruction, on campus in library and information science programs, and on or off campus in continuing education programs. Courses in abstracting are given at many universities and colleges that offer library or information science programs. The courses often include training in indexing. Continuing education short courses in abstracting, sponsored by universities, governmental agencies, or private enterprises, are given infrequently on and off campus.

Many free-lance abstractors teach themselves to abstract by using guidelines provided by data base or information services. This training normally consists of a short period of reading and familiarization with the objectives and instructions of a particular abstracting system, followed by the actual writing of abstracts in conformance with system instructions. Some on-the-job training programs include a short pretraining period involving proofreading or minor editing tasks to assist the abstractor candidate in gaining familiarity with the style and content of abstracts. Staff editors or senior abstractors instruct the trainees and monitor their progress until the required level of proficiency is achieved.

No matter what level or type of training an abstractor receives, what supervisors at three major data base producers state about the development of indexers is equally true for abstractors: "Learning by practicing and doing it and getting comments on your work is the best way to learn how to index." (Tenopir, 1992, p. 18)

VOLUNTEER ABSTRACTORS

Once a good source of specialized abstracts, the ranks of volunteer abstractors are steadily decreasing in number and output. Rowlett (1980) reports that *Chemical Abstracts* began publication in 1907 with 129 volunteer abstractors who presumably prepared almost all of the 11,847 abstracts published that year. The number of volunteer abstractors for this publication increased steadily to a peak of 3,292 in 1966, when they prepared 67 percent of the abstracts that the Chemical Abstracts Service (CAS) published that year.

In 1979, some 1,000 volunteer abstractors wrote approximately 10 percent of the abstracts for *Chemical Abstracts*. Most of the remaining 90 percent of the more than 500,000 abstracts were produced in a single intellectual review of the documents, using online computer-assisted aids, at CAS offices in Columbus, Ohio or at CAS associates in Nottingham, England.

Rowlett predicts a continuing decline in assignments for volunteer abstractors, a situation that may well be typical of all information processing systems that use or have used the services of these abstractors. He concludes, nevertheless, that the dedicated service of volunteer abstractors probably always will be required in some difficult subject areas and for documents in the less common languages.

CHAPTER 21

Apologetic or Confident Abstractors

Five years ago I was almost apologetic. A lot has changed since then.

—FRANK BORMAN
Former President, Eastern Airlines (1981)

Back in 1976, Frank Borman, as an ex-astronaut who had been the command pilot of the Apollo 8 spacecraft on the first lunar orbital mission, had little to be apologetic about. But as president of one of the leading commercial airlines, he was then feeling "almost apologetic" because "it was no secret that our service needed improving." By 1981, the airlines advertising copy from which he is quoted proclaimed that a top-to-bottom effort at improving services within the company enabled Borman to boast, "I'll stack our service up against anyone's."

More than 12 years ago, when my thoughts for writing the first edition of this book were still in the embryo stage, besides the positive comments that I heard from some fellow abstractors about the value of abstracting and the satisfaction to be found in writing abstracts, I heard a few comments from others which suggested that they felt "almost apologetic" that they were making their living as abstractors.

For a few well-qualified abstractors with many years of experience, the apologetic note may have stemmed from frustration over delays in moving on to more advanced writing or editing assignments. Some may not have been convinced that abstracting is a fully professional use of

159

their education and skills. Others may have felt apologetic because they were aware that they were not writing abstracts expediently, but did not have the will or desire to improve. These abstractors were figuratively marking time, while waiting for a computer program or a neural network to write their abstracts for them automatically.

Other than some of the content in Borko and Bernier's (1975) monograph on abstracting concepts and methods and Ashworth's (1973) paper on the joys of achievement associated with abstracting, abstractors who may have turned to the literature on library and information science for stimulating materials on the subject of abstracting probably would have found little that is encouraging.

In their guide to information science, Davis and Rush (1979) even speculate on whether humans are really capable of writing good abstracts:

> Little is known about how or why human abstractors choose from the original article what they include in the abstracts that they produce. Neither is it clear to what extent human abstractors are consistent in abstract production. Perhaps more important, especially since there is no concrete answer to the question of what constitutes a good abstract, questions relating to human selection and consistency may be irrelevant. It is just possible that the abstracts produced by humans are not good. If so, then it would be undesirable to try to emulate the processes that humans use in abstracting, since such emulation would lead simply to a faster rate of production of consistently poor abstracts, which might be easy to produce, but difficult to sell. (pp. 40–41)

I disagree with the speculation that abstracts composed by humans are inherently not good. But I do agree with Davis and Rush's implication that there is much room for improvement.

SELF-STARTING AND INNOVATIVE ABSTRACTORS

What kind of abstractor performance is worth emulating? Two of my favorite appraisal terms for good performance are "self-starting" and "innovative." Self-starters and innovators regularly begin their work promptly, do it effectively, and resolve most of the problems they encounter in the process. When they are stymied they seek expert advice. Experienced abstractors freely give advice when it is requested and are knowledgeable enough to do so; if not, they attempt to make referrals to the best possible alternative sources.

More specifically, I would apply the terms "self-starting" and "innovative" to those abstractors who follow this advice: When abstracting, observe all the rules of analytical reading, particularly those for self-editing and revising, by means of value-to-meaning reading. (Too many abstractors fail to do the latter.) When instructed to write an original abstract for a paper, monograph, or report that already contains an author abstract or summary, do so, and ignore the author abstract.

Those who do not follow this advice are prone to producing "original" abstracts that resemble the authors' versions far too closely in style and content. But those who do follow this advice frequently are pleased to find that the specialized skills that they have developed as professional abstractors allow them to write abstracts that are more informative than the authors', having a structure and style that conforms closely to the specifications of the publisher or sponsor of the information system for which they are writing abstracts.

Finally, I advise both author and documental information processing abstractors to construct well-construed abstracts (not merely extracts) that would please such advocates of abstracts as Koestler (1980), who had this to say about abstracts and extracts in the introduction to his essay "The Art of Discovery and the Discoveries of Art":

> It is technically difficult and sometimes impossible to convey a complex theory by quoting extracts from the original text. The alternative is to condense and summarise—to abstract rather than extract. (p. 344)

Appendix 1

Abstract of the *American National Standard for Writing Abstracts*[1]

An abstract is an abbreviated, accurate representation of the contents of a document, preferably prepared by its author(s) for publication with it. Such abstracts are also useful in access publications and machine-readable data bases. The following recommendations are made for the guidance of authors and editors, in order that the abstracts published in primary documents may be both helpful to the readers of these documents and reproducible with little or no change in access publications and services. If changes are required, however, many of the guidelines presented should prove useful.

Prepare an abstract for every formal item in journals and proceedings, and for each separately published report, pamphlet, thesis, monograph, and patent. Make the abstract as informative as the nature of the document will permit, so that readers may decide, quickly and accurately, whether they need to read the entire document. State the purpose, methods, results, and conclusions presented in the original document, either in that order or with initial emphasis on findings (results and conclusions).

---

[1]This material is reproduced with permission of the American National Standards Institute (ANSI) from the *American National Standard for Writing Abstracts,* ANSI Z39.14.1979, copyright 1979 by ANSI. No form of this standard excerpt may be reproduced without the prior written consent of ANSI. Copies of the full text of this standard may be purchased from ANSI, 11 West 42nd Street, New York, NY 10018.

Place the abstract as early as possible in the document, with a full bibliographic citation on the same page. Make each abstract self-contained, since it must be intelligible without reference to the document itself. Be concise without being obscure; retain the basic information and tone of the original document. Keep abstracts of most papers and portions of monographs to fewer than 250 words, abstracts of reports and theses to fewer than 500 words (preferably on one page), and abstracts of short communications to fewer than 100 words.

Write most abstracts in a single paragraph, except those for long documents. Normally employ complete, connected sentences; active verbs; and the third person. Use nontextual material such as short tables and structural formulas only when no acceptable alternative exists. Employ standard nomenclature, or define unfamiliar terms, abbreviations, and symbols the first time they occur in the abstract.

When abstracts are employed in access publications and services, precede or follow each abstract with the complete bibliographic citation of the document described. Include pertinent information about the document itself (type; number of tables, illustrations, and citations) if this is necessary to complete the message of the abstract; here, complete sentences need not be used.

Appendix 2

Suggested Reading Rules
for Learning
How to Write Abstracts

GENERAL READING RULES FOR ABSTRACTING

Rule 1. Read actively to identify information for the abstract and passively for understanding.

Rule 2. Read with standard rules and conventions and special instructions for writing abstracts in mind.

Rule 3. Read attentively and enthusiastically through the full abstracting process of reading, writing, self-editing, and revising.

ANALYTICAL READING RULES FOR ABSTRACTING

The following suggested reading rules were primarily formulated for use in learning how to prepare purpose- or findings-oriented informative abstracts, indicative abstracts, or combined indicative–informative abstracts. With minor adjustments, however, they are easily adaptable for use in learning how to prepare such other forms as structured abstracts.

Exploratory-to-Retrieval Reading

There are two rules for this form of reading, which ideally should be done once, nonstop, with a minimum of regressions and fixations. In practice, however, it may be necessary to repeat portions of this reading process.

Rule 1. Scan exploratively the text of the material to be abstracted to identify passages containing information having potential for retrieval for inclusion in the abstract.

Rule 2. While scanning, mentally or in the margin of the copy, note those parts of the material that contain information on purpose, methods, findings, or conclusions and recommendations.

Responsive-to-Inventive Reading

In this stage, and guided by four rules, the potentially extractable information that was identified in the exploratory-to-retrieval reading stage is responsively weighed for its potential to be inventively written into the abstract.

Rule 1. *(Step A)* Reread all of the information on purpose, scope, and methods (aboutness) that you identified during the exploratory-to-retrieval reading process. While reading, mentally index the primary and secondary themes that were described in this candidate material for the abstract, using your own choice of arbitrary terms or phrases. (Beginning abstractors or those writing an abstract for a complex document might find it helpful to jot down any arbitrary index terms or phrases on note paper.) *(Step B)* Write the primary aboutness part of the abstract (the first sentence).

Rule 2. If there is any other information on aboutness that you think is relevant to the abstract, write an additional sentence or sentences. If your instructions call for an indicative abstract, you have now completed the responsive-to-inventive reading stage and are ready to begin the value-to-meaning reading stage for self-editing of the completed abstract. If, however, you are writing an informative abstract, continue on to Rules 3 and 4, or to Rule 4 only, if you are writing an indicative–informative abstract.

Rule 3. *(Step A)* If you are writing an abstract for a document reporting on experimental research, tests, surveys, clinical case reports, or similar studies, reread the textual materials on the results or findings. While reading, condense this information mentally, or write it on note paper, to aid your judgment of its relevance and significance. *(Step B)* Inventively extract the most relevant results and write them in sentence form, concisely, in descending order of significance.

Rule 4. *(Step A)* If the abstract does not already exceed word limitations, reread the conclusions and recommendations, if any, that were identified during the exploratory-to-retrieval reading process, as described in Rule 3. *(Step B)* Extract the most relevant conclusions and recommendations and write them in sentence form, tersely, in descending order of significance, to the full extent that space for the abstract remains.

Connective (Value-to-Meaning) Reading

There are five suggested rules for the self-editing or revising of draft abstracts via connective reading—two for value adding and three for meaning making. Novice abstractors are advised to follow the rules separately in sequence. Normally, experienced abstractors should have no difficulty applying most of the rules simultaneously during a single analytical reading of the text of their draft abstracts.

INTRINSIC VALUE ADDING

Rule 1. Is the abstract properly structured and unified?

Rule 2. Is the content of the abstract coherent and concise?

MEANING MAKING

Rule 3. After scanning the text of the document being abstracted, is it clear that the fullest amount of meaning feasible has been represented in the draft abstract?

Rule 4. Does this abstract conform fully with standard abstracting guidelines or those of the sponsoring abstracting service, journal publisher, or data base vendor?

Rule 5. Are there any other problems with the style or content of the draft abstract that might be resolved expediently by consulting with other abstractors, editors, technical reviewers, or subject experts, as available and appropriate?

Appendix 3

Abstracting Style Points

In the citations that follow, after the style point headings (e.g., **Abbreviations** 2:10–11; 8:129), the number preceding the colon represents one of the eight references. For each style point, the elaborative entries in the right column are extracted from one or two of these references, as indicated in superscripts.

References:
1. American National Standards Institute, Inc. *American National Standard for Writing Abstracts*. New York, American National Standards Institute, Inc., 1979. ANSI Z39.14.1979
2. Borko, H., and C. L. Bernier. *Abstracting Concepts and Methods*. San Diego, Calif., Academic Press, 1975.
3. Borko, H., and S. Chatman. "Criteria for Acceptable Abstracts: A Survey of Abstractors' Instructions." *American Documentation, 14*(2):149–160, 1963.
4. Collison, R. L. *Abstracts and Abstracting Services*. Santa Barbara, Calif., A. B. C.-Clio, 1971.
5. Lancaster, F. W. *Indexing and Abstracting in Theory and Practice*. Champaign, Ill., University of Illinois, Graduate School of Library and Information Science, 1991.
6. Maizell, R. E.; J. F. Smith; and T. E. R. Singer. *Abstracting Scientific and Technical Literature: an Introductory Guide and Text for Scientists, Abstractors, and Management*. New York, Wiley-Interscience, 1971.
7. Rowley, J. E. *Abstracting and Indexing*. 2nd ed. London, Eng., Clive Bingley Limited, 1988.

8. Weil, B. H.; I. Zarember; and H. Owen. "Technical-Abstracting Fundamentals. II. Writing Principles and Practices." *Journal of Chemical Documentation,* 3(2):125–132, 1963.

Style points:	*Extracts*
Abbreviations 2:10–11 8:129	Ad hoc abbreviations may be used by abstractors for long words repeated several times in an abstract. Such abbreviations are given in parentheses after the first occurrence of the name in full and are thereafter used consistently throughout the abstract.[2] Use standard abbreviations for physical units and commonplace words. Heavy use of abbreviations is an obvious way of shortening an abstract, but it is one that slows reading considerably.[8]
Author's wording 5:98	Some abstractors feel that they must change the words of an author. While paraphrase is frequently necessary to achieve brevity, nothing is gained by changing the author's words in striving for originality.[5]
Accuracy 1:9 2:11–12 5:97–98 6:210	Reducing the number of errors to the barest minimum is a necessary, although expensive, goal of the abstracting service. . . . Omissions are the most serious kind of error, for the user cannot be expected to detect what isn't there. Content errors can be reduced in number by instructing and training the abstractor. Feedback is essential, as is editorial alertness.[2]

Ambiguity *see* **Clarity**

Articles 8:130	Avoid both overusing and awkward omission of articles, e.g., "Pressure is a function of temperature," not "The pressure is a function of the temperature," but "The refinery operated . . .," not "Refinery operated . . ."[8]
Brevity 2:9–11, 68–70 4:13	All natural languages, such as English, are full of redundancy, much of which can be eliminated during abstracting of the original docu-

5:97–98
6:78
7:26

ment. Abstract users read abstracts knowing that they must be alert to every word, and they must, in places, read in reasonable surmises. . . . Descriptions of well-known techniques, equipment, processes, conclusions, premises, axioms, and results—common knowledge, what one educated or trained in the fields is expected to know—are commonly omitted from abstracts. . . . What the investigator tried to do but did not accomplish, and what he intends to do next, while perhaps important in the original article, are generally omitted from the abstract as a matter of policy.[2]

Clarity
2:13
5:97–98
6:210

The abstract is clear and unambiguous. Trade names, jargon, acronyms, and the like, are either adequately explained or not used at all.[6]

Colloquialisms
8:130

Use trade jargon and colloquialisms sparingly and carefully. Although jargon can give an authentic flavor to an abstract, its use has pitfalls. The same jargon words may mean different things in different fields, or nothing at all, except to a very few readers.[8]

Conciseness
2:21–24
6:80–81
7:27

Redundant phrases such as: "the authors studied," "in this work," "the paper concludes by," "this can be taken to indicate that," "these discussions lead to the recommendations that," should be avoided if at all possible. . . . Never use a clause where a briefer phrase will do, or a phrase where one word will suffice.[7] He (the abstractor) does not waste words. He avoids repetitive and meaningless expressions. He knows that superlatives and other adjectives are not usually necessary.[6]

Consistency
4:52–53
6:6

An abstractor cannot be expected to cover everything thoroughly—to do so would defeat the purpose of the abstract. Also, most abstractors write in a way that reflects their training, experience, and interests, no matter how objective they try to be. Users should know about this "built-in" limitation of abstracts.[6]

Extracting
2:21, 162–163
6:77

The abstractor can attempt to paraphrase in concise form what the author of the original document has said. But he[/she] will often want to retain as much as possible of the original emphasis and terminology for the sake of accuracy. He[/she] may want to use brief direct excerpts to prevent changing meanings because of any subjective leanings he[/she] may have or because of excessive zeal for compactness.[6]

Jargon *see* **Clarity, Colloquialisms**

Length *see* **Brevity**

Paraphrasing *see* **Extracting**

Point of view
3:18

There is often a close correlation between one's notion of the function of abstracts and his[/her] rhetorical point of view; in informative abstracts, the abstractor will be completely identified with the author, while in descriptive abstracts, the abstractor will stand apart, behind locutions like "X was attempted" or "The author believes Y."[3]

Punctuation
2:74

Punctuation in abstracts is the same as in any good prose form. . . . Complete sentences and abbreviations (except those of units of measurement) have periods. Commas are used to separate members of a series, and a comma is placed just before the conjunction connecting the last two members of a series. Semicolons are used for combining closely related sentences into one sentence and for separating parts of series in which commas are used within one or more of the parts.[2]

Redundancy *see* **Brevity**

Symbols *see* **Abbreviations**

Synonyms 8:130	Avoid the overuse of synonyms that can lead to absurd-sounding phrases—the so-called "sin of synonyms." We would not say "The resin exchanges potassium ions for *basic electrolytes*." We would simply be content with ". . . hydroxyl ions," despite the repetition of "ions."[8]
Telegraphic writing 2:74	A telegraphic style is undesirable. A few beginning abstractors may write this way in the hope of saving space. Complete sentences and only authorized abbreviations should be used.[2]

Terseness *see* **Conciseness**

Verb tense 3:17 8:129	The past tense is used in describing experimental work, including the procedure, equipment, conditions, theoretical bases, and data obtained. The present tense is used in giving conclusions derived from the experimental data.[3]
Voice 1:10 3:16 8:129	Use verbs in the active voice whenever possible; they contribute to clear, brief, forceful writing. However, the passive voice may be used for indicative statements and even for informative statements in which the receiver of the action should be stressed.[1]

Appendix 4

Select Annotated
Bibliography on Abstracting

Annotations that are adapted from abstracts in *Information Science Abstracts* (*ISA*) are appended with the *ISA* accession number for the modifed abstract, for example, *ISA*, 77-1462.

QUALITY

Ashworth, W. "Abstracting as a Fine Art." *Information Scientist,* 7(2):43–53, 1973.

> Abstracting is discussed as an activity requiring creativity and skill and having a susceptibility to formal analysis. Abstracts prepared with good literary style serve a useful purpose in improving communication while providing a source of creative fascination to the abstractor.

King, R. A. "A Comparison of the Readability of Abstracts with Their Source Documents." *Journal of the American Society for Information Science,* 27(2):118–121, 1976. *ISA,* 75-3396

> The readability levels of 30 items from child development abstracts and 30 passages from their corresponding journal articles were compared by a CAL SNOBOL computer program referenced to a CLOZE criterion. Results support the hypothesis that abstracts were more difficult to read than their source documents.

Kowitz, G. T., et al. "From ERIC Source Documents to Abstracts: A Problem in Readability." Presented at the Rocky Mountain Education Research Association, Tucson, Ariz., November 29, 1973. *ISA,* 77-2174

> The Flesch RE formula was used to calculate readability scores for abstracts and their source documents, which were selected randomly from the clearinghouses. An analysis of variance indicated that the abstracts were readable, but less so than the source documents.

Tenopir, C., and P. Jasco. "Quality of Abstracts." *ONLINE, 17*:44–55, May 1993.

> The consistency of style and readability, the extent to which the ANSI standard is observed, and the informativeness of the abstracts in three periodical indexes on CD-ROM were tested.

GUIDELINES

Borko, H., and S. Chatman. "Criteria for Acceptable Abstracts: A Survey of Abstractors' Instructions." *American Documentation, 14*(2):149–160, 1963.

> Instructions in 130 guides for abstractors were reviewed to develop criteria for judging the adequacy of human-produced abstracts initially and computer-produced abstracts subsequently, if necessary. An adequate abstract of a research article must cover purpose, method, results, conclusions, and specialized content.

McGirr, C. J. "Guidelines for Abstracting." *Technical Communication, 5*(2):2–5, 1978.

> Advice on the preparation, review, content, and length of abstracts is presented. Abstracts should use definite statements, not generalities; short clear statements for each thought; and language familiar to the reader.

Weil, B. H.; I. Zarember; and H. Owen. "Technical-Abstracting Fundamentals. II. Writing Principles and Practices." *Journal of Chemical Documentation, 3*(2):125–132, 1963.

> Guidelines are presented for writing findings- (reader-) oriented informative abstracts. Abstracts can serve their purpose best only

if they are carefully written to transmit important information to readers quickly and accurately, which requires knowledge of audience needs, habits, and desires, and the ability to identify the key facts in the document, to organize these facts, and to write the abstracts clearly, concisely, and in conformity with the style rules of the medium involved.

MONOGRAPHS

Borko, H., and C. L. Bernier. *Abstracting Concepts and Methods.* San Diego, Calif., Academic Press, 1975. *ISA,* 77–1325

The history, production, organization, and publication of abstracts are discussed. Instructions, standards, and criteria for abstracting are considered, along with information on management, automation, and personnel in terms of possible economies that can be derived from the introduction of new technology or management techniques.

Cleveland, D. B., and A. D. Cleveland. *Introduction to Indexing and Abstracting.* 2nd ed. Englewood, Colo., Libraries Unlimited, 1990.

The fundamentals of indexing and abstracting are presented as a foundation for entry-level professional practice. Discussions begin with the basic concepts of information and its bibliographic control, then cover abstracting and indexing methods, and conclude with a section on their professional aspects.

Collison, R. L. *Abstracts and Abstracting Services.* Santa Barbara, Calif., A. B. C.-Clio, 1971. *ISA,* 72-1627

The mechanical production of abstracts, from abstractor to finished, edited, and indexed abstract, is described.

Lancaster, F. W. *Indexing and Abstracting in Theory and Practice.* Champaign, Ill., University of Illinois, Graduate School of Library and Information Science, 1991.

Intended primarily for use in schools of library and information science, the text stresses the similarities between indexes and abstracts as published by abstracting and indexing services (in paper or electronic form). The text is also intended for individuals and institutions involved in information retrieval, including librarians, managers of information centers, and data base producers.

Maizell, R. E.; J. F. Smith; and T. E. R. Singer. *Abstracting Scientific and Technical Literature: an Introductory Guide and Text for Scientists, Abstractors, and Management.* New York, Wiley-Interscience, 1971. *ISA,* 72-2147

A practical guide on the writing, dissemination, and use of scientific and technical abstracts. The guide includes information on managing abstracting operations within a company or organization, the role of the abstractor in literature searching, and how an abstractor can use modern technology to facilitate the production and use of abstracts.

Rowley, J. E. *Abstracting and Indexing.* 2nd ed. London, Eng., Clive Bingley Limited, 1988.

Key practices in the fields of abstracting and indexing are described; central practices are highlighted to lay a foundation for more advanced studies; and an integrated view of manual and computerized retrieval systems and abstracting products is offered.

COMPUTATIONAL ABSTRACTING

Black, W. J. "Knowledge-based Abstracting." *Online Review, 14*(5):327–337, 1990.

Progress is reviewed for the production of rule-based abstracts by extracting content-indicative sentences and aggregating some of them into a coherent text.

Borkowski, C. "Structure, Effectiveness and Benefits of LEXtractor, an Operational Computer Program for Automatic Extraction of Case Summaries and Dispositions from Court Decisions." *Journal of the American Society for Information Science, 26*(2):94–102, 1975. *ISA,* 75-2226

A computer program (extractor) for automatic extraction of case summaries and dispositions is described. The structure of LEXtractor, its cost and performance, and relevant issues in text editing are outlined.

Craven, T. C. "A Computer-aided Abstracting Tool Kit." *Canadian Journal of Information and Library Science, 18*(2):19–31, 1993.

> Prototyped computerized abstracting assistance in a text network management system that includes sentence weighting on stems in a passage or on lists of cue words; adjusting weights of segments; and weighting on frequency stems. The minimum length of extracts, threshold for a frequent word/stem, and sentence weights are adjustable.

_____ . "Graphic Display of Larger Sentence Dependency Structures." *Journal of the American Society for Information Science, 42*(5):323–331, 1991.

> Qualities are outlined for graphic representation of sentence dependency structures in texts longer than a few sentences. Prototyped TEXNET experimental text structure management is discussed, along with automatic structure simplification and the addition of dummy sentences.

_____ . "Use of Words and Phrases from Full Text in Abstracts." *Journal of Information Science, 16*(6):351–358, 1990.

> The extent to which human abstractors actually extract words, phrases, and possibly longer sequences from the original full texts was preliminarily investigated, along with the relationship between the length of the original document and the length of the abstract and the positions of extracted words and phrases within full texts. A small, but significant, tendency for abstract words and phrases to concentrate at the beginning of the full text was observed.

_____ . "A Coding Scheme as a Basis for the Production of Customized Abstracts." *Journal of Information Science, 13*(1):51–58, 1987.

> A method for obtaining independently meaningful abstracts from a single intermediate representation is outlined, and preliminary results with software designed to implement this method are considered. The essential idea is the linking of anaphoric expressions to their antecedents—the fuller designations of the things to which they refer.

Kuhlen, R. "Some Similarities and Differences Between Intellectual and Machine Text Understanding for the Purpose of Abstracting." In: *Representation and Exchange of Knowledge as a Basis of Information Processes*. Edited by H. J. Dietschmann. North-Holland, Neth., Elsevier Science Publishers, B. V., 1984, pp. 87–107.

> Analysis of abstracting rules for German working systems reveals that no method exists, as yet, for real machine simulation of intellectual text abstracting, owing to differences in machine and human analysis and condensation techniques. Knowledge-based textual analysis and processing is needed. Abstracting rule-based requirements are formulated for an automatic abstracting system.

Mathis, B. A. *Techniques for the Evaluation and Improvement of Computer-Produced Abstracts*. Columbus, Ohio, Ohio State University, The Computer and Information Science Research Center, 1972. OSU-CISRC-TR-79-15; *ISA*, 73-1644

> An automatic abstracting system (ADAM), implemented on an IBM 370, receives journal articles as input and produces abstracts as output, using an algorithm that considers all of the sentences in the input text and rejects those which are not suitable for inclusion in the abstract.

Oldfield, D. E. "Document Abstracting on the Distributed Array Processor." In: *Supercomputers and Parallel Computation*. Edited by D. J. Paddon. Oxford, Eng., Oxford University Press, 1984, pp. 135–145.

> A method of automatic abstracting is described for which a parse is first performed. The syntactic category of each word is encoded into a bit-significant 64-bit code, which can be manipulated by simple logical operations and reduces data movements to logical shifts.

Paice, C. D. "Constructing Literature Abstracts by Computer: Techniques and Prospects." *Information Processing and Management*, 26(1):171–186, 1990.

> Early and recent progress in automatic construction of abstracts is reviewed, with emphasis on how to produce coherent, balanced, and stylistically acceptable ones and the use of abstract frames to ensure proper coverage and balance.

Prikhod'ko, S. M., and E. F. Skorokhod'ko. "Abstracting from Analysis of Links Between Phrases." *Nauchno-Tekhnicheskaya Informatsiya, Seriya 2, 16*(1):55–65, 1982.

> Semantic links between sentences in a text were analyzed, and an algorithm was tested involving text input, compilation of a word list, formation of a repetition dictionary, calculation of sentence weights, ranking sentences, selecting sentences, and printing them out.

STRUCTURE OF AND CONTENT IN ABSTRACTS

Arndt, K. A. "The Informative Abstract." *Archives of Dermatology, 128*(1):101, 1992.

> This article reports that abstracts in *Archives of Dermatology* will be structured into three sections: background and design; results; and conclusions (clinical and laboratory studies) and background, observations, and conclusions (observations).

Broer, J. W. "Abstracts in Block Diagram Form." *IEEE Transactions on Engineering Writing and Speech, 14*(3):64–67, 1971. *ISA,* 72-1626

> A block diagram of interconnected word blocks, with standardized titles and located in fixed positions of a two-dimensional information space, contains condensed answers to what, how, and why. The arrangement aims at improving similarity between verbal structure and logical organization and at stimulating further work via multichannel input-output.

Herner, S. "Subject Slanting in Scientific Abstracting Publications." In: *International Conference on Scientific Information, Washington, D.C., Proceedings*. Vol. 1. Washington, D.C., National Academy of Sciences–National Research Council, 1959, pp. 407–427.

> Abstracts from 51 scientific periodicals that were announced in 9 indexing and abstracting publications were analyzed to determine the feasibility of cooperative abstracting. Statistical analysis of papers having no author summaries or abstracts indicates that subject slanting of abstracts is rare.

Lancaster, F. W., and S. Herner. "Modular Content Analysis." *Proceedings of the American Documentation Institute, 27th Annual Meeting, October 1964.* Vol. 1. Washington, D.C., American Documentation Institute, 1964, pp. 403–405.

Full content descriptions of documents that result in an annotation; indicative, informative, and critical abstracts; and a set of modular index entries are proposed. The descriptions would eliminate duplication and waste of intellectual effort and furnish a product of standardized format.

Liddy, E. D. "The Discourse-level Structure of Empirical Abstracts: An Exploratory Study." *Information Processing and Management,* 27(1):57–81, 1991.

Broadening the research reported below, knowledge structures of experts in abstracting, the linguistics of a sample of abstracts, and a model of the structure of empirical abstracts were studied. Results suggest that a predictable discourse-level structure exists in empirical abstracts, which is similar to the abstractors' internalized structure for them; also, lexical cues indicate the presence of the structural components.

_____ . "Discourse-level Structure in Abstracts." *Proceedings of the Annual Meeting of the American Society for Information Science.* Vol. 24. Medford, N.J., Learned Information, 1987, pp. 138–147.

Components and the relations among them were studied in abstracts for educational and psychological research. Components are those categories of text content that define the text type; relations are properties that hold between two or more entities and define the type of interaction, influence, or co-occurrence that hold between them.

Manning, A. D. "Abstracts in Relation to Larger and Smaller Discourse Structures." *Journal of Technical Writing and Communication,* 20(4):369–387, 1990.

A unified theory of discourse structure is proposed to explain why textbooks consistently recognize just two polar types of abstracts; why students often produce adequate descriptive abstracts and short paraphrases of text, but not adequate summary abstracts; and how a short paraphrase differs formally and conceptually from a summary abstract.

Rennie, D., and R. M. Glass. "Structuring Abstracts to Make Them More Informative." *Journal of the American Medical Association,* *266*(1):116–117, 1991.

Authors of articles for *JAMA* describing clinical trials and other preplanned clinical investigations and authors of review articles are instructed on how to prepare structured abstracts. The structure reminds authors, reviewers, and editors of the necessity for providing each category of information.

Salager-Meyer, F. "Discoursal Flaws in Medical English Abstracts: A Genre Analysis per Research- and Text-type." *Text, 10*(4):365–384, 1990.

The discourse structure (headings such as "purpose," "scope," and "findings") was examined for fundamental medical text types (research papers, case reports, and review articles) and basic research types (clinical, basic, epidemiological, and operative).

Trawinski, B. "A Methodology for Writing Problem Structured Abstracts." *Information Processing and Management, 25*(6):693–702, 1989.

Problem-structured abstracts contain five parts: document problem, problem solution, testing method, related problems, and content elements. Content element symbols (e.g., DEF, definitions of concepts; SCO, scope of document) denote the presence of types of information in the document.

Vaughan, D. K. "Abstracts and Summaries: Some Clarifying Distinctions." *The Technical Writing Teacher, 18*(2):132–141, 1991.

Abstracts and summaries can be confused with each other because they share a number of similarities: position in the document, brevity, conciseness, and content. Essential aspects of the two forms were analyzed. These include purpose, reader, tone, logic, relation to the parent document, and length.

STANDARDS

Tibbo, H. R. "Abstracting Across the Disciplines: A Content Analysis of Abstracts from the Natural Sciences, the Social Sciences, and the Humanities with Implications for Abstracting Standards and Online Information Retrieval." *Library and Information Science Research,* *14*(1):31–56, 1992.

Comparison of content categories (purpose, scope, conclusions, etc.) listed in abstracting standards with the content of abstracts in the sciences, social sciences, and humanities indicate that, although the standards reflect the abstracting practices of scientists, they do not match those in the field of history. Implications of the findings for online free-text retrieval are noted.

INFORMATION RETRIEVAL

Fidel, R. "Writing Abstracts for Free-text Searching." *Journal of Documentation, 43*(1):11–21, 1988.

Data base critera for acceptability of abstracts for free-text searching were surveyed to determine the degree to which existing abstracting and indexing services already incorporate such criteria into their abstracting. Characteristics of abstracts important to free-text retrieval are synthesized.

Liddy, E. D.; S. Bonzi; J. Katzer; and E. Oddy. "A Study of Discourse Anaphora in Scientific Abstracts." *Journal of the American Society for Information Science, 38*(4):255–261, 1987.

Occurrences of discourse anaphora (abbreviated subsequent references, exemplified by, but not limited to, pronouns) in abstracts were analyzed, and rules were developed for algorithms of the decisions made by human processors on whether a term is an anaphor and what is its referent.

Appendix 5

Little Summary, Big Summary
on Summaries of Text

summary—A report that is lacking in details. (p. 534)

—CHARLES J. and ROGER J. SIPPL (1984)

LITTLE SUMMARY ON SUMMARIES OF TEXT

The Sippl's (1984) brief definition of "summary" in the third edition of their *Computer Dictionary* is an example of a very "little summary" of what a summary is within the lexicon of computers.

Abstracts are examples of summaries of documents or text that are sometimes confused with each other, as will be discussed shortly. Summaries of written texts, or oral presentations such as lectures, take many forms. These include "little" summaries such as annotations, paraphrases, and epitomes and big summaries, including actual summaries, abstracts, precis, synopses,[1] gists, and digests. As indicated in the next section, several of these forms are sometimes defined as synonymous.

Because of this relatedness of forms, the guidelines—specifically for producing abstracts in the full text of this book—should also have extensive relevance for the production of all other forms of summaries.

---

[1]Definitions of precis and synopses are given in the Glossary.

185

BIG SUMMARY ON SUMMARIES

Domains of research in which summarization is studied include scientific and technical documentation and information retrieval. Extensive research on summaries also is carried on in psychology and in the teaching fields, where summaries are used as training tools in learning how to read, write, and listen and how to appreciate imaginative works.

Definitions

Summaries have been defined as follows in guidelines on writing in general and scientific and technical writing in particular, and in discussions of language and education.

WRITING (GENERAL)

"A summary (or abstract or precis) is your condensation of what someone else has written." (Flynn and Glaser, 1984, p. 388).

WRITING (SCIENTIFIC)

"The summary tells readers what happened in your research. In short, the summary gives away the show right from the beginning and allows readers to decide quickly whether they want to read your paper." (Alley, 1987, p. 138).

LANGUAGE

"A comprehensive and usually brief abstract or digest of a text or statement." (McArthur, 1992, p. 1005). "A summary is a 'condensation of the substance of a work.' It is a concise statement containing the premise of a subject as well as its conclusions: 'His fine *summary* of the course gave us new insights.' The briefest possible summary of the essential points of a work is called an *epitome* (Greek *epi*, 'upon,' *temnein*, 'to cut'); hence to cut short." (Freeman, 1983, pp. 284–285).

EDUCATION

"A summary is an expanded main idea statement for the selection, expressing the general ideas that the writer would like the reader to remember—the 'gist' of the writing." (Thistlewaite, 1991, p. 26). "By definition, a summary must capture the gist of a piece as well as reduce the material substantially. The ability to create summaries develops slowly, and even many high school and adult students have difficulty with this skill." (King, 1992, p. 305). "A summary is a condensed version, in your own words, of the writing of someone else, a condensation that reproduces the thought, emphasis, and tone of the original. It abstracts all the significant facts of the original—overall thesis, main points, and important supporting details—but, unlike a paraphrase, it omits and/or condenses amplifications such as descriptive details, digressions, anecdotes, illustrations, and repetitions." (McAnulty, 1981, p. 50).

Summaries in Scientific and Technical Documentation

Vaughan (1991) defines two primary kinds of summaries within technical documentation: concluding and executive. The former follow sections of the text, summarize important points, and "are an invaluable feature in textbooks and instruction manuals." Prefatory executive summaries describe the problem discussed, its implications, available solutions, and the preferred solution.

Vaughan also draws the following distinctions, among others, between executive summaries and informative abstracts: The abstract is characterized by a detached tone, while the summary is written with a slight persuasive edge. The abstract follows a procedural or chronological sequence, whereas the summary follows a cause-and-effect sequence. The abstract represents the original document and should be thought of as functioning separately from it; while the summary accompanies or precedes the report. Also, according to Vaughan, the informative abstract typically is between 250 and 500 words long; while the executive summary is typically from 2 to 10 pages long.

Confusion Between Abstracts and Summaries

In the literature on scientific and technical documentation, Manning (1990) and Purcell (1990), in attempting to clarify some of the confusion in descriptions of abstracts and summaries, also may have added unwittingly to it. While discussing the relationship between larger and smaller discourse structures, Manning examines definitions and the typology of abstracts, particularly summary (informative) and descriptive (indicative) ones. He explains "how a summary abstract differs in principle from a short paraphrase of an article" (p. 369) and "why students often can produce adequate descriptive abstracts, and short paraphrases of texts, but . . . often do not produce adequate summary abstracts." (pp. 384–385)

Purcell prefers using the phrase "abstract summary" instead of just the word "abstract," because "Apparently, in shortening a useful phrase [abstract summary] to a single term, the second word 'summary' got dropped rather than the first word 'abstract.' It seems that a phrase like 'abstract summary'—a summary which has been pulled, or extracted, from a document—has been shortened to the adjective 'abstract,' although any intellectual information is abstract, or intangible." (p. 358)

Text Processing and Summarization for Information Retrieval

Rau, Jacobs, and Zernick (1989) describe the text processing, language, and summarization components of the prototype information retrieval System for Conceptual Information Summarization, Organization and Retrieval (SCISOR). They apply two methods to solve the problem of a lack, in natural-language systems, of "rich enough lexicons to cover all the important words and phrases in extended texts." (p. 419) The methods comprise the use of text processing that is "tolerant of unknown words and gaps in linguistics knowledge" and acquiring "lexical information automatically from the texts." (p. 419) The authors conclude that their "integration of extensive text processing capabilities with automated language acquisition and a summarization algorithm forms a practical strategy for providing conceptual information retrieval in limited domains." (p. 428)

Cognitive and Educational Psychology

In their influential study on psychological processes and condensation rules in text comprehension and the production of recall and summarization protocols, Kintsch and van Dijk (1978) describe microprocesses for the gisting of information in a text base. The summarizer relates incoming information to that which he or she already has from the text, context, or general knowledge of the system. During the production of summaries, textual information is reduced coherently to a gist via deletions and inferences.

Augmenting Kintsch and van Dijk's condensation rules for summarizing texts, Brown and Day (1983) studied groups of subteen- and teenage students, junior college students, and graduate students who had taught a freshman rhetoric course. As applied to the summarization of expository text, their rules called for the deletion of trivial or redundant text, the substitution of a superordinate (generalized) term for a list of items or actions, and the selection or invention (construction) of topic sentences for paragraphs. The results of Brown and Day's study indicated that the older students performed better at rearranging text across paragraphs and at writing synopses. The younger and junior college students experienced the most difficulty in selecting or inventing topic sentences for the summaries.

In Sherrard's (1985) paper, "The Psychology of Summary Writing," the preceding and related studies on summarization are reviewed. Among other results from her survey, Sherrard cites Kieras and Bovair's (1981) finding that "abstraction of the main idea from simple technical prose can be carried out without deep understanding, to the extent that a computer can accomplish it." (p. 256)

Ruddell and Boyle (1989) studied the effects of cognitive mapping on the comprehension and written summarization of text by freshmen college students. Such maps are described as representations of text that facilitate "integration and retention of information by providing the reader with a cognitive scheme to reconstruct meaning." (p. 13) The mapping process apparently enhanced the understanding of complex text patterns and added to the students' procedural knowledge for the effective organization of information for summarization. Mapping students used significantly more "cohesive ties" (such as, because, therefore, in contrast) as signals for relationships among propositions than did nonmapping students.

Three groups of college students in a remedial reading and study skills course listened to lectures and took notes and then generated and answered their own questions on the lecture content, wrote summaries of the lectures, or reviewed their lecture notes (King, 1992). Using their notes and recalling from memory, the summarizers wrote a main topic sentence for the lecture, then wrote several linking sentences for subtopics and other main ideas. King determined that, at immediate posttesting, summarizers recalled more of the lecture content than did self-questioners and notetaking reviewers. One week later, the self-questioners retained "somewhat" more of the lecture content than the summarizers and significantly more than the notetaking reviewers. King also found that the lecture notes of the self-questioners and summarizers contained more ideas from the lecture than did those of the notetaking reviewer students.

Teaching Summarization

> Writing summaries promotes thinking and learning across the curriculum—but why are they so difficult to write? (Hill, 1991, p. 536)

Hill (1991) concludes that writing summaries is difficult, primarily because of difficulties in text content and its organization, "followed by degree of [the student's] comprehension, availability of text [while the summary is being written], audience [oneself or others], intended purpose, type of summary required, genre [whether the text is a simple narrative or is expository], and text length." (p. 537) Also, summary writing requires the ability to abstract. Learning to write summaries is a long process, in which "beginning instruction should be based on writing summaries of a narrative structure with a time-ordered format." (p. 539)

While teaching summarization skills to high school students, Hare and Borchardt (1984) introduced rules for combining text from different paragraphs and for "polishing" rough versions of summaries. These rules supplement those for deleting trivia and redundancies, generalizing lists of items, and selecting or inventing a topic sentence. Ways of polishing the summaries include paraphrasing, using connecting words, and inserting introductory or closing statements. Direct instruction involved explicit outlining of the component processes of the teaching strategy and developing lessons to teach them.

Following the method of Duffy and Roehler (1982), the strategy was either "deductive, proceeding from general rules to deducing particulars, or inductive, proceeding from particulars to inducing general rules." (p. 64) Post-instruction, experimental high school students did significantly better than control students in summarization efficiency and rule usage at and two weeks after instruction. The ability to identify implicit topic sentences did not improve.

Based on metacognitive processes for determining the main ideas in text, Jacobowitz (1990) developed "A strategy for constructing the Author's Intended Message" (AIM) (Figure 8). Guiding undergraduate students "to rely on their own knowledge and skills to comprehend what they read," the strategy promotes their self- and task knowledge and self-monitoring. AIM combines skills for establishing the "purpose, prereading, activation of background knowledge, prediction, determination of text organization, and critical evaluation into one study strategy." (p. 622)

Teaching methods for improving comprehension and summarization of text or information are primary themes in two papers published in the April 1987 issue of the *Journal of Reading*. Carr and Ogle (1987) use their "K-W-L reading-thinking strategy," which includes text mapping [outlining] and summarizing information, to teach remedial and other high school students how to improve their independent reading skills. Components of K-W-L are: recalling what is **K**nown; determining what students **W**ant to know; and identifying what is **L**earned. Using a worksheet, before reading, the students first brainstorm ideas and discuss the topic to recall background knowledge; next, they categorize what they have recalled and anticipate other categories of information that they may find during reading, before generating questions they may want answered as they read. Additional questions and new information can be added to the "want to know" and "what is learned" sections of the worksheet, respectively, as the students do the actual reading. Postreading, they discuss what they have learned while reading. Summarizing "requires students independently to reflect on what was learned, to write in a logical and comprehensible manner, and to express what was learned in their own terms." (p. 629) With the aim of transferring what they have learned using the K-W-L, mapping, and summarization strategy to other reading tasks, students are encouraged to use this strategy independently while being given corrective feedback from their teachers.

There are certain questions you can ask before, during, and after reading a selection that may help you figure out the author's message or main idea. These questions may be applied to any text (any content). They will serve to establish purposes for your reading and get you more involved with the material. (It is helpful to jot down brief answers to these questions as you proceed. You may find that some questions are more useful than others, depending on what you are reading.)

Before reading

1. What is the topic of the selection? How much do I know about this topic? Is this topic a controversial one for me? Do I have any feelings about the topic?

2. What do I expect to find out about this topic? What are some questions that may be answered as I read?

3. Who is the author? Have I read anything by this person? Do I know anything about this author that may help me understand the message?

During reading

4. Has the author provided an introduction to the selection that tells what the major points will be? Can I paraphrase the introduction?

5. As I read, do I see any words or phrases that signal any particular organizational pattern (such as comparison/contrast, cause/effect)? If yes, can I construct a tentative main idea that reflects the pattern?

6. Does the author draw any conclusions or provide a summary that can help me to determine the intended message?

7. Did I predict appropriate purpose questions before I read? Can I answer any at this point? What other purpose questions can I ask now as I read?

After reading

8. What do I think the author's purpose was in writing this material? Does it match my purpose for reading? If not, what questions did the author answer? Do I agree with the author's opinion or conclusion?

9. Am I able to paraphrase or summarize the material? Are there headings and subheadings that I can use to help me do this?

10. What can I do if I still haven't determined the AIM? (reread, skim, look at my purpose questions again, ask other questions, discuss with a classmate)

Figure 8 AIM: **A strategy for constructing the Author's Intended Message.** SOURCE: T. Jacobowitz. "AIM: A Metacognitive Strategy for Constructing the Main Idea of Text." *Journal of Reading, 33*(8):620–624, 1990. Reprinted by permission of the author.

For the effective transfer and independent use of strategies for comprehension, Gambrell, Kapinus, and Wilson (1987) advocate that students be taught how to process text using mental imagery during reading and how to reorganize text by summarizing following the reading. Mental images "provide a framework for organizing and remembering information from text, and when students induce images, they expend more energy on integrating information across text." (p. 639) Teachers should begin instruction in mental imagery by stating words to the effect: "Today we will concentrate on making mental images, or pictures, about what we read. Mental imagery is a reading strategy that helps you comprehend what you're reading." (p. 639) They should then explain why mental imagery is useful, demonstrate the strategy, conduct guided practice, then provide text for independent practice. Summarizing can also be taught using teacher modeling and guided and independent practice. The authors conclude that "The first step is to convey the characteristics of a good summary. It is brief, it has the important ideas of a passage, and it does not include supporting details." (p. 641)

Appendix 6

Responsive-to-Inventive Reading for Sample Abstract A (Continued from Chapter 8)

PURPOSE, SCOPE, AND METHODS

[Paragraph 2] Forrester, a professor at M.I.T.'s Sloan School of Management, relies on a computer model he developed to simulate the growth, decline, and stagnation of a hypothetical city (or "urban area") from birth to old age (250 years). . . . In his first chapter Forrester warns the reader that caution should be exercised in applying the model to actual situations. Subsequently, however, he expresses few reservations about the model's validity and freely uses it as a basis for prescribing public policy. [INDEX TERMS: computer model; simulation; urban growth/decline; public policy]

[Paragraph 3] The hypothetical city in *Urban Dynamics* is, in Forrester's words, "a system of interacting industries, housing, and people." At the start of the simulations there is only new industry in the city, but as time passes enterprises mature and then decline. The speed of this aging process depends on conditions in the city. As businesses pass through these successive stages, they employ fewer workers and a smaller proportion of skilled workers. [INDEX TERMS: industries; housing; workers]

[Paragraph 4] There are similarly three kinds of people in the city: "managerial-professional," "labor" (skilled or high-income workers), and "underemployed" (including unemployed and unskilled workers). And there are three kinds of housing, corresponding to the three kinds of people: premium housing, worker housing, and underemployed housing. [INDEX TERMS: management; employment; industries; housing; workers]

[Paragraph 5] The criteria used in evaluating the performance of the hypothetical city and the efficacy of alternative public policies are never explicitly set forth. However, minimization of taxes per capita would be a fair rendering of the underlying criteria. Forrester seems to think that the objective of the city is to produce the lowest possible tax rate. [INDEX TERMS: performance evaluation; taxes; supply side fiscal policy]

[Paragraph 6] The fiscal relationships in Forrester's urban system are intricate, but can be reduced to three fairly simple propositions: (1) Low-income households cost the city more in taxes than they pay, whereas the city makes a profit on high-income households. (2) Growing business enterprises are an unqualified good because they pay taxes and, by assumption, cost the city nothing in services. (3) Increases in local taxes and increases in local government expenditures produce "adverse" changes in the city's population and employment structure. It follows from these propositions that "urban-management policies" should be designed to encourage new enterprises and managerial-professional people to locate in the city and discourage low-skilled people from living there. [INDEX TERMS: financing; income; taxes; management planning]

[Paragraph 7] The influence of tax rates on employment and population structure in Forrester's city is powerful and pervasive. "Managerial-professional" and "labor" families are assumed to be repelled by high tax rates, whereas the "underemployed" are indifferent to them. High tax rates, moreover, discourage the formation of new enterprises and accelerate the aging of existing ones. There are still other adverse effects: high taxes retard construction of both premium and worker housing, which in turn discourages the kinds of people who live in these kinds of housing from moving to the city or remaining there. [INDEX TERMS: taxes; effects; employment; population; housing]

[Paragraph 8] Increases in public expenditures, the other half of the local fiscal equation, also have disastrous effects on the system. It is assumed that increases in expenditures per capita make the city no more attractive to high-income people and new enterprises, but make it substantially more attractive to low-income people. There are some small offsets in the positive effects of higher expenditures per capita on upward mobility from the underemployed class into the labor class; but these are overwhelmed by the direct and indirect effects on the size of the underemployed population. [INDEX TERMS: public financing; mobility; employment]

[Paragraph 9] These examples are only a few of the "adverse" consequences of higher taxes and increased public expenditures in Forrester's model. Since the model is so constructed that a development in one sector affects other sectors, these adverse effects cumulate throughout the system. [INDEX TERMS: taxes; public financing]

[Paragraph 10] Forrester uses his simulation model to evaluate several "urban-management programs" that have been tried or proposed, and he concludes that they "may actually worsen the conditions they are intended to improve." For example, he finds that "financial support from the outside"—presumably, including revenue sharing by the federal government—"may do nothing to improve fundamental conditions within the city and may even worsen conditions in the long run." But this conclusion is not at all surprising in view of what he does with the outside funds. Rather than using them to reduce or hold down city taxes, as proponents of such intergovernment transfers envision, Forrester uses them to increase city expenditures. Given the framework of his model, the net effects are inevitably adverse. [INDEX TERMS: computer model; evaluation; urban models; financing, external; taxes; municipal expenditures]

[Paragraph 11] But Forrester considers only the favorable effects of the demolition program. Given his model, these are considerable. The induced shortage of low-income housing makes the city less attractive to low-income people; fewer come and more leave. (Where they go is a question the model is not designed to consider.) As before, a decline in the ratio of "underemployed" to total population makes the city more attractive to high-income people, encourages formation of new enterprises and construction of premium and worker housing, and impedes deterioration of dwelling units and businesses. In addition, the land cleared by increased demolition of low-income housing provides space for new enterprises and for premium and worker housing. [INDEX TERMS: taxes; costs; housing; mobility; employment; urban decline]

CONCLUSIONS/RECOMMENDATIONS

[Paragraph 2] Before adequate models become available, many inadequate ones will be put forward. Forrester's model is a conspicuous example. [INDEX TERM: inadequate model]

[Paragraph 10] If instead Forrester had used the outside support to reduce city taxes, the net effects would have been favorable to the hypothetical city. Virtually all of Forrester's evaluations of "conventional" policies are similarly flawed; none is a faithful rendering of policies it supposedly represents. [INDEX TERM: inferior evaluation of municipal fiscal policies]

[Paragraph 11] Considering the heavy emphasis Forrester puts on tax rates, it is striking that he fails to consider the costs of his principal recommendation: each year demolish 5 percent of the low-income housing. The costs of acquiring and demolishing the properties would increase city taxes, and, within the framework of the model, any increase in city taxes has adverse effects. But Forrester considers only the favorable effects of the demolition program. [INDEX TERM: failure to include cost of annually demolishing a percentage of low-income housing]

[Paragraph 12] Given the critical role of land availability in the model, it would appear that these adverse effects could be staved off if the city could simply extend its boundaries so as to absorb additional vacant land; but Forrester does not deal with this possibility. [INDEX TERM: failure to predict use of vacant land beyond city limits]

[Paragraph 13] Simplification is essential in computer simulation models, and neither Forrester's nor any other model can be criticized merely because it omits detail. But Forrester omits some basic behavioral relationships. The model's most serious weakness is that the suburbs never explicitly appear in it. For some simulation purposes, it might be permissible to disregard temporarily the interrelations between, say, the city and the rest of the nation beyond the metropolitan area. But what happens in a city strongly influences its suburbs, and vice versa. If the central city reduced its low-income population by 100,000, the low-income population of the suburbs would have to increase by roughly the same amount. Although Forrester's model reflects no awareness of this aspect of metropolitan interdependence, suburban governments are all too aware of it. Indeed, much of the urban problem today is a result of suburban governments' successfully pursuing precisely the kind of begger-thy-neighbor policies Forrester advocates for the central city. [INDEX TERM: no explict mention of reciprocal urban and suburban effects]

[Paragraph 14] Upon scrutiny, *Urban Dynamics* amounts to an intricate attempt to justify the responses of big-city mayors to a harsh fiscal environment. Existing intergovernmental arrangements saddled them with awesome responsibilities for the nation's social problems, but failed to provide them with commensurate financial resources. Much of the mayors' enthusiasm for now much-criticized urban-renewal programs is traceable to their desperate need for cash. In *Urban Dynamics,* pragmatic responses to an unbalanced allocation of responsibilities and tax resources are elevated to the status of rational and efficient policies for dealing with the complex web of problems popularly referred to as the "urban crisis." [INDEX TERM: misinterpretation of significance of pragmatic financing of urban renewal programs]

[Paragraph 15] The solution is not, as Forrester indicates, the pursuance of narrow self-interest by each local government. Instead we need to develop a more appropriate division of responsibilities and functions among governments, and thereby remove the fiscal incentives for local governments to follow policies that, while perhaps efficient from the viewpoint of narrow self-interest, are inefficient from the viewpoint of society as a whole. [INDEX TERM: recommend redistribution of municipal responsibilities and functions]

Appendix 7

Responsive-to-Inventive Reading for Sample Abstract B (Continued from Chapter 9)

PURPOSE, SCOPE, AND METHODS

[Paragraph 3] If the same ratio of *cis*-epoxide to aldehyde obtained from the *cis*-3-hexene is maintained in the *trans*-3-hexene products, the residual aldehyde presumed to arise from the *trans* intermediate may be calculated. . . . This factor was used to calculate the ketone residual from the *cis* complex, starting with the *cis*-4-octene. [INDEX TERMS: *cis-trans* isomerism; aldehydes; olefins; residuals; calculations]

[Paragraph 5] A direct comparison between methyl and ethyl migrations is desirable if their relative rates are to be established; this can be done through the use of 3,4-dimethyl-3-hexene (DMH). . . . Both *cis*- and *trans*-3,4-dimethyl-3-hexene were used. The two ketone products, 4,4-dimethyl-3-hexanone and 3-ethyl-3-methyl-2-pentanone, will be referred to as I and II. The use of 3-ethyl-2-methyl-2-pentene (MEP) furnishes further data for assessing the validity of the concept of relative rates of migration of groups in establishing the product ratios. [INDEX TERMS: group migration; hydrogen atoms; methyl groups; ethyl groups; *cis-trans* isomerism; product ratios]

[Paragraph 6] Reactions were effected at 90°K in the apparatus routinely used for this purpose. The olefins were diluted 10 to 1 with propane. The exposure time to oxygen atoms was 5 min, and about 1% of

201

the olefin was reacted. The products were determined, after warmup, on a column (0.25 in. × 12 ft glpc) of Carbowax-6000, at 135° and a helium flow of 100 cc/min. The *cis* and *trans* isomers of 3,4-epoxy-3,4-dimethylhexane were not separable. Ketones I and II were easily separable. Retention times were determined with authentic samples of the two ketones. [INDEX TERMS: reactions; low temperature; olefins; oxygen addition; *cis-trans* isomers; retention time]

[Table I] Fractional Product Yields for the O(^{3}P) Addition to Internal, Straight-Chain Olefins at 90°K . . . Products . . . 2-Butene, 2-Pentene, 3-Hexene, 4-Octene . . . *trans*-Epoxide, *cis*-Epoxide, Aldehyde, Ketone, *trans*-Epoxide/ketone, *cis*-Epoxide/aldehyde, *cis*-Epoxide/*trans*-epoxide. Total epoxide/total carbonyl. . . . The olefins were diluted 10:1 in propane prior to condensation on a 100-cm^2 Pyrex surface. Sum of 2-propylpentanal and *cis*-4,5-epoxyoctane, not separated on the gas-liquid chromatography. [INDEX TERMS: fractional product yields; oxygen addition; straight-chain olefins; low temperature; epoxides; aldehydes; ketones; *cis-trans* isomerism; dilution; condensation; gas-liquid paper chromatography]

RESULTS

[Paragraph 2] Comparison of the *trans*-epoxide to ketone ratios from the *cis-* *vs.* the *trans*-olefin with increasing size of the olefin indicates that these ratios diverge. However, the larger olefins show greater stereospecificity in their reactions. Thus, *cis*-3-hexene gives about 2.5 times as much *cis*-3,4-epoxyhexane as the *trans*-epoxide. [INDEX TERMS: *trans*-epoxide to ketone ratios diverged; greater stereospecificity for larger olefins]

[Paragraph 6] For all three olefins, only three gas-liquid paper chromatography peaks were obtained for the products. These corresponded to the epoxides and the ketones I and II. [INDEX TERM: olefin gas-liquid paper chromatography peaks corresponded to epoxides and ketones]

CONCLUSIONS

[Paragraph 2] Even a relatively small quantity of 3-hexanone from the *cis* intermediate could easily account for the difference in the *trans-*

epoxide/ketone ratio between the reactions of *cis*- and *trans*-3-hexene. It is noted that the recently proposed "epoxide-like" transition complex implies that, although only one form of the complex is possible from the *trans*-, two forms are possible from the *cis*-olefin. . . . Of these, form b could readily lead to the ketone, because of easy migration of H, but form a would be expected to preponderate from the energetic viewpoint. [INDEX TERM: effect of 3-hexanone on *trans*-epoxide/ketone ratio]

[Paragraph 3] An indication of the importance of these forms, within the framework of the transition states specified and the assumption that form a gives only the aldehyde in its rearrangement to the carbonyl end product, whereas form b gives mostly ketones, is obtained from the data of Table I. . . . Clearly, aldehyde formation from the *trans* intermediate is negligible. All of the straight-chain olefins of Table I conform to this generalization. . . . The correct value, 2.3, is obtained from *trans*-4-octene, because a contribution from the *cis* complex possible is virtually absent. . . . Although the *cis*-epoxide and aldehyde were not separated, the ratio of the two may be assumed to be the same as the corresponding one from *cis*-3-hexene. . . . It may be concluded that of the two forms of the transition complex derived from the *cis*-olefin, form a is the principal one and b is unimportant. [INDEX TERM: negligible aldehyde formation from *trans* intermediate for all straight-chain olefins]

[Paragraph 4] Two generalizations are apparent from Table I. The first is that retention of configuration of products becomes more pronounced with increasing chain length of the olefin. The second is that reaction of oxygen atoms in the low-temperature region tends to be more stereospecific with *trans*- than with *cis*-olefins. A stereotransformation of the transition intermediate requires a rotation of 180°, about the modified olefinic bond, of one of the carbon atoms of the double bond with its attached groups. Obviously, this process occurs with the *cis*-olefins. The extent to which stereotransformation will occur depends on the rates of ring closure and the rates of rearrangements leading to final products, compared to the rate of *cis-trans* interchange in the complex. It seems reasonable to postulate that the rate of ring closure is independent of the size of the olefin. The ratio of total epoxide to total carbonyl products shows little change with size, and, hence, the rate of rearrangement to carbonyls is also size independent. The frequency of rotation of the portion of the complex . . . is then directly proportional to the extent of stereotransformation observed in the products. A measure of these transformations is the ratio of *cis*- to *trans*-epoxide, tabulated in Table I. . . . Qualitatively, it would be expected that because of the higher moment of inertia associated with the larger olefin, the stereospecificity should increase with size; this is indeed the case. It is interesting that *cis*-2-pentene shows more stereospecificity than *cis*-2-butene. Despite the fact that both compounds have a methyl group adjacent to the olefinic site, a larger rotational barrier is inferred to be associated with the 2-pentene. A quantitative consideration of the relationship of size and stereo effects would require that potential barriers for rotation be taken into account also, but the qualitative conclusions remain unaffected. [INDEX TERMS]: retention of configuration of products with increasing olefin chain length; oxygen atom reactions more specific with *trans* olefins; stereotransformation of transition intermediate; stereotransformation and ring closure; rearrangement to carbonyls; stereospecificity increases with size]

[Paragraph 5] (The same two ketones are produced from MEP as from *cis*- and *trans*-DMH.) The important difference is that, whereas I results from the reactions of DMH with a rearrangement wherein a methyl group migrates, it is the migration of the ethyl group that gives I from MEP. . . . Therefore, if independent rates of migration are to be associated with these alkyl groups, the ketone ratio (I/II) produced from *cis*- or *trans*-DMH should be equal to (II/I) formed from MEP. It is emphasized that this follows if the presumed migration rates determine the position at which the O becomes localized. On the other hand, strong forces favoring addition to one of the olefinic carbons could control the alkyl group migrations. [INDEX TERM: addition to olefinic carbons and migration of alkyl groups]

[Paragraph 7] The notable feature of these results is that, of the two ketones, I and II, I is the major product: (I/II) = 2.5:1. Furthermore, this ratio is virtually independent of the starting olefin. Thus, the concept of independent rates of migration of groups in the rearrangement occurring in the O atom addition to olefins *must be abandoned*. The other alternative would require that the directive effect of the alkyl groups in MEP is such that the O adds to the carbon with the two ethyl groups 2.5 times more rapidly than to the carbon with the two methyl groups. It would appear that, insofar as the ratio of ketones is concerned, it is their relative stabilities that control the rearrangement processes. Transformation to final products is a migration of an alkyl group concerted with the localization of the oxygen atom on one of the carbon atoms. Localization of the oxygen atom in the transition complex *preceding* alkyl group rearrangement is not in accord with the experimental results. If, in fact, localization did occur, the migration would be determined, in part (completely, if, as in MEP, the groups bonded to each of the olefinic carbon atoms occurred in pairs), by the directive factors, such as electron densities that are postulated as controlling the site of addition. . . . For MEP, addition of the O atom to that carbon atom of the double bond to which the two methyl groups are attached would be expected to be favored. Ketone II would, perforce, be formed in greater amounts than I; the data show unequivocally that this is incorrect. [INDEX TERMS: no independent group migration rates in rearrangements from O addition to olefins; ketone stability and control of rearrangement processes; final products via alkyl group migration and localization of oxygen atom on carbon atom]

[Paragraph 8] The concerted rearrangement, in which oxygen localization and group migration occur, requires both electronic and spatial reorganization. The addition of ground-state, triplet oxygen to singlet-state olefin to give singlet-state products requires a relaxation process, as represented by a crossing of states on a potential surface. The recently introduced representation of the initial transition intermediate as a loose epoxide structure seems especially appropriate. Migration of groups probably involves a transient bridging of the double bond carbon pair. The path by which the intermediate relaxes to final products could even involve steric effects. The formation of the grouping . . . in II is sterically less favorable than . . . in I, and it may be speculated that the preponderance of I over II in the reactions of the *cis-* and *trans-* DMH and MEP can be ascribed to such steric effects. [INDEX TERMS: electronic and spatial reorganization; transient bridging; steric effects]

[Paragraph 9] Table II shows an interesting variation among the three olefins as regards the epoxide/ketone ratio. The interpretation of these results, and, particularly, why MEP exhibits such a high epoxide/ketone ratio, is not yet at hand. [INDEX TERM: epoxide/ketone ratios]

Glossary

The authors and dates that appear in parentheses are keyed to the References section at the end of the book and indicate that the definition is based on or was extracted from a definition in the cited work.

aboutness information (abstracting) Information in the text on purpose, scope, and methodology with potential for inclusion in the indicative or descriptive components of abstracts. Inclusion of information from other specific aboutness categories (e.g., hypotheses, subjects, implications, or relation to other studies) may be prescribed by particular publishers or abstracting services.

abridgements *See* **summaries**

access abstracts Collections of abstracts that are prepared for access publications, such as abstract (secondary) journals, and computer-based information retrieval systems.

annotations One or two sentence notations or explanations of the content of documents or studies.

author abstracts Published initially in primary publications; they are normally, but not exclusively, written by the authors of the published materials and are usually either informative or indicative. Author abstracts are frequently redistributed (intact or revised), copyright permitting, by access information services.

automatic abstracts *See* **computational abstracts**

compendia or **compendiums** *See* **summaries**

computational abstracts Composed, partially or fully, by using techniques for computer-assisted selecting, extracting, formatting, and printing of representative information.

critical abstracts Contain evaluative comments that are deliberately added by the abstractors on the significance of the material abstracted or the style of its presentation.

descriptive abstracts *See* **indicative abstracts**

documental information processing (abstracting) Mental representation of elements or components of information in the text into abstracts; this contrasts with computational information processing of text into abstracts by programming computers to select or reject sentences.

epitomes *See* **summaries**

extracts Unedited representative portions of a document, usually in sentence form; used as basic materials for composing abstracts or as substitutes for them.

findings-oriented abstracts Informative abstracts that contain major results, conclusions, and/or recommendations in a topical first sentence, followed by sentences that contain further results, conclusions or recommendations, and supporting details on methodology, purpose, or scope (American National Standards Institute, Inc., 1979; Weil, Zarember, and Owen, 1963b). *See also* **purpose-oriented abstracts**

highlight abstracts Used by editors of journals to inform readers more fully about the contents of articles in scientific, technical, and scholarly journals (Mathis, 1972).

indicative abstracts Prepared from discursive or descriptive forms of text, including essays, discussions, arguments, descriptions, editorials, reviews, narratives, biographies, and bibliographies. Contain information about the purpose, scope, and occasionally the methodology of the discussions or descriptions represented in the text of the document being abstracted.

indicative–informative abstracts Contain purpose-like information, similar to that found in indicative abstracts, that is, combined with conclusion-like statements. Such statements may take the form of straightforward conclusions or be associated with opinions, judgments, recommendations, suggestions, implications, evaluations, applications, new relationships, or hypotheses accepted or rejected.

information processing (abstracting) *See* **documental information processing (abstracting)**

informative abstracts Prepared from texts describing experimental investigations, inquiries, or surveys. Contain key results, conclusions, recommendations, opinions, or interpretations, which are normally preceded in the abstract by aboutness information on purpose, scope, or methodology.

meaning making (abstracting) Abstractors attempt to ensure that, within the constraints of the time and space allotted, as much as possible of what the writer intended to express or indicate in the document being abstracted and the intended sense of the writer's words have been represented in the abstract. The meaning-making processes draw on the abstractor's problem-solving and decision-making skills, such as reasoning, judging, deducting, inducting, extrapolating, analyzing, and synthesizing.

modular abstracts Full content descriptions of documents prepared by subject specialists that result in an annotation; indicative, informative, or critical abstracts; and a set of modular index entries. Designed to eliminate duplication and waste of intellectual effort and to furnish a product of standardized format for partial or complete use by a variety of access services (Lancaster and Herner, 1964).

precis *See* **summaries**

professional relationships (cooperative) Process through which abstractors, editors, reviewers, managers and sponsors of information systems, and users contribute to or monitor and advise on methods for developing and maintaining the highest standards of quality for the composition of abstracts, within the constraints of time and money.

purpose-oriented abstracts Abstracts in which information on the primary objectives, scope, or methodology is presented before the details of results, conclusions, recommendations, opinions, or interpretations. *See also* **findings-oriented abstracts**

reading (analytical, for abstracting) Done to construct well-construed informative or indicative abstracts that reflect clear thinking and concise, coherent, well-balanced writing of relevant information.

rules (abstracting) Control the style and content of abstracts; they are based on guidelines in standards, specifications, instructions, or style manuals of primary publishers or sponsors and managers of access abstracting services, as supplemented by general style points in manuals for lengthier forms of scientific, technical, and scholarly writing.

scope   Intent and import of a writing or discourse (Borko and Bernier, 1975).

structured abstracts   Information in the abstract is given using prescribed headings; introduced into segments of the medical literature, for example, for descriptions of clinical trial reports (heading samples: "Objective," "Design," or "Patients or Other Participants") or reviews (heading samples: "Objective," "Data Sources," or "Study Selection").

summaries   Besides its synonymity with the term abstract, the term summary and its related terms (abridgement, precis, synopsis, etc.) often are defined almost interchangeably. In his *Treasury for Word Lovers,* Freeman (1983, p. 285) makes a commendable, if not entirely successful attempt to differentiate the meanings of these terms. Extracts from some of his definitions under the heading "Summary and Related Words" follow.

  abridgement   a shortening of a large work, such as a book or treatise, by selecting the most important portions.

  compendium   a brief compilation.

  epitome   briefest possible summary of the essential points of a work; more often than not, *epitome* is wrongly used to mean "high point."

  precis   "a statement of the gist"; it is an abstract, and is more suitably used of small works—a passage, a chapter, or a report.

  synopsis   a summary presented as an outline or a list of headings, sometimes of a work in progress or of a text to be presented in the future; according to its Greek forebear (*syn*, "together"; *opsis*, "view"), a general view, a viewing all together.[1]

synoptics   Concise publication in a journal that presents the key ideas and results of a full-length article; includes an abstract, diagrams, references, etc; is refereed; and the full-length article is either published,

---

[1]SOURCE: Morton S. Freeman. *A Treasury for Word Lovers.* Extracts from "Summary and Related Words." Philadelphia, Pa., ISI Press, 1983, p. 285. Reprinted with permission of the author.

elsewhere or subsequently, or is made available from a repository (ANSI, 1979). [Presently is more prevalent in Europe than in the United States.]

value adding (abstracting)   Quality check of draft abstracts to screen out errors in style and content and add such attributes as unity, diversity, coherence, conciseness, brevity, clarity, and consistency to their intrinsic value.

References

Adler, M. J. (Editor in Chief), and W. Gorman (General Editor). *The Great Ideas: A Syntopicon of Great Books of the Western World.* 2nd ed. 2 vols. Chicago, Ill., Encyclopaedia Britannica, 1990.

Adler, M. J., and C. Van Doren. *How to Read a Book: the Classic Guide to Intelligent Reading.* New York, Simon and Schuster, 1972.

Alley, A. *The Craft of Scientific Writing.* Englewood Cliffs, N.J., Prentice Hall, 1987.

American National Standards Institute, Inc. *American National Standard for Writing Abstracts.* New York, American National Standards Institute, Inc., 1979. ANSI Z39.14.1979

Arndt, K. A. "The Informative Abstract." *Archives of Dermatology, 128*(1):101, 1992

Ashbery, J. *As We Know.* New York, The Viking Press, 1963.

Ashworth, W. "Abstracting as a Fine Art." *Information Scientist, 7*(2):43–53, 1973.

Beghtol, C. "Bibliographic Classification Theory and Text Linguistics: Aboutness Analysis, Intertextuality and the Cognitive Act of Classifying Documents." *Journal of Documentation, 42*(2):84–113, 1986.

Berthoff, A. E. *Forming, Thinking, Writing: the Composing Imagination.* New York, Hayden Book Company, 1978.

Black, W. J. "Knowledge-based Abstracting." *Online Review, 14*(5):327–337, 1990.

Borko, H., and C. L. Bernier. *Abstracting Concepts and Methods.* San Diego, Calif., Academic Press, 1975.

Borko, H., and S. Chatman. "Criteria for Acceptable Abstracts: A Survey of Abstractors' Instructions." *American Documentation, 14*(2):149–160, 1963.

Borkowski, C. "Structure, Effectiveness and Benefits of LEXtractor, an Operational Computer Program for Automatic Extraction of Case Summaries and Dispositions from Court Decisions." *Journal of the American Society for Information Science, 26*(2):94–102, 1975.

Broer, J. W. "Abstracts in Block Diagram Form." *IEEE Transactions on Engineering Writing and Speech, 14*(3):64–67, 1971. *ISA,* 72-1626

Brown, A. L., and J. D. Day. "Macrorules for Summarizing Texts: The Development of Expertise." *Journal of Verbal Learning and Verbal Behavior, 22*(1):1–14, 1983.

Bruner, J. *Acts of Meaning.* Cambridge, Mass., Harvard University Press, 1990.

Brusaw, C. T.; G. J. Alred; and W. E. Oliu. *Handbook of Technical Writing.* 4th ed. New York, St. Martin's Press, 1993.

Carr, E., and D. Ogle. "K-W-L Plus: A Strategy for Comprehension and Summarization." *Journal of Reading, 30*(1):626–631, 1987.

Chapman, R. L., ed. *Roget's International Thesaurus.* 5th ed. New York, HarperCollins, 1992.

Ciardi, J. *Dialogue with an Audience.* Philadelphia, Pa., J. B. Lippincott, 1963.

Cleveland, D. B., and A. D. Cleveland. *Introduction to Indexing and Abstracting.* 2nd ed. Englewood, Colo., Libraries Unlimited, 1990.

Collison, R. L. *Abstracts and Abstracting Services.* Santa Barbara, Calif., A. B. C.-Clio, 1971.

Craven, T. C. "A Computer-aided Abstracting Tool Kit." *Canadian Journal of Information and Library Science, 18*(2):19–31, 1993.

_____ . "Graphic Display of Larger Sentence Dependency Structures." *Journal of the American Society for Information Science, 42*(5):323–331, 1991.

_____ . "Use of Words and Phrases from Full Text in Abstracts." *Journal of Information Science, 16*(6):351–358, 1990.

_____ . "A Coding Scheme as a Basis for the Production of Customized Abstracts." *Journal of Information Science, 13*(1):51–58, 1987.

Cremmins, E. T. "Information Retrieval Diary of an Expert Technical Translator." *ASIS Bulletin, 10*(1):25–26, 1984.

Davis, C. H., and J. E. Rush. *Guide to Information Science.* Westport, Conn., Greenwood Press, 1979.

Day, R. A. *How to Write and Publish a Scientific Paper.* 2nd ed. Philadelphia, Pa., ISI Press, 1983.

Duffy, G. G., and L. R. Roehler. "Commentary: The Illusion of Instruction." *Reading Research Quarterly, 17*(3):438–445, 1982.

Farradane, J. E. L. "Relational Indexing. Part I." *Journal of Information Science, 1*(5):267–276, 1980a.

_____ ."Relational Indexing. Part II." *Journal of Information Science, 1*(6):313–324, 1980b.

_____ . "Knowledge, Information, and Information Science." *Journal of Information Science,* 2(2):75–80, 1980c.

_____ . "The Nature of Information." *Journal of Information Science,* 1(1):13–17, 1979.

_____ . "Towards a True Information Science." *The Information Scientist,* 10(3):91–101, 1976.

_____ . "Concept Organization for Information Retrieval." *Information Storage and Retrieval,* 3(4):297–314, 1967.

_____ . "The Psychology of Classification." *Journal of Documentation,* 11(4):187–201, 1955.

Farrow, J. F. "A Cognitive Process Model of Document Indexing." *Journal of Documentation,* 42(2):149–166, 1991.

Fidel, R. "Writing Abstracts for Free-text Searching." *Journal of Documentation,* 43(1):11–21, 1988.

Flynn, J., and J. Glaser. *Writer's Handbook.* New York, Macmillan Publishing, 1984.

Freeman, M. S. *A Treasury for Word Lovers.* Philadelphia, Pa., ISI Press, 1983.

Gambrell, L. B.; B. A. Kapinus; and R. M. Wilson. "Using Mental Imagery and Summarization to Achieve Independence in Comprehension." *Journal of Reading,* 30(7):638–642, 1987.

Great Books of the Western World. 2nd ed. Chicago, Ill., Encyclopaedia Britannica, 1990.

Gregory, R. L., ed. *The Oxford Companion to the Mind.* Oxford, Eng., Oxford University Press, 1987.

Grudin, R. *The Grace of Great Things: Creativity and Innovation.* New York, Ticknor & Fields, 1990.

Guston, P. *Catalog of an Exhibition Held at the San Francisco Museum of Modern Art and Other Museums, May 16, 1980–September 13, 1981.* San Francisco, Calif., San Francisco Museum of Modern Art, 1980.

Hare, C. V., and K. M. Borchardt. "Direct Instruction of Summarization Skills." *Reading Research Quarterly,* 20(1):62–78, 1984.

Herner S. "Subject Slanting in Scientific Abstracting Publications." In: *International Conference on Scientific Information, Washington, D.C., Proceedings.* Vol. 1. Washington, D. C., National Academy of Sciences–National Research Council, 1959, pp. 407–427.

Hill, M. "Writing Summaries Promotes Thinking and Learning Across the Curriculum—But Why Are They So Difficult to Write?" *Journal of Reading,* 34(7):536–539, 1991.

Jacobowitz, T. "AIM: A Metacognitive Strategy for Constructing the Main Idea of Text." *Journal of Reading,* 33(8):620–624, 1990.

James, W. "The Energies of Men." In: *Essays on Faith and Morals.* Selected by R. B. Perry. New York, Longmans, Green, 1947, pp. 216–237.

Just, M. A., and P. A. Carpenter. *The Psychology of Reading and Learning to Read.* Boston, Mass., Allyn and Bacon, 1987.

Kain, J. F. "A Computer Version of How a City Works." *Fortune, 80*(6):241–242, 1969.

Kieras, D. E., and S. Bovair. *Strategies for Abstracting Main Ideas from Simple Technical Prose.* Tuscon, Ariz., University of Arizona, Psychology Department, November 10, 1981. Technical Report No. UARZ/DP/TR-81/9

King, A. "Comparison of Self-Questioning, Summarizing, and Notetaking-Review as Strategies for Learning from Lectures." *American Education Research Journal, 29*(2):303–323, 1992.

King, R. A. "A Comparison of the Readability of Abstracts with Their Source Documents." *Journal of the American Society for Information Science, 27*(2):118–121, 1976.

Kintsch, W., and T. A. van Dijk. "Toward a Model of Text Comprehension and Production." *Psychological Review, 85*(5):363–394, 1978.

Klein, R., and M. D. Scheer. "Addition of Oxygen Atoms to Olefins at Low Temperature. IV. Rearrangements." *Journal of Physical Chemistry, 74*(3):613–616, 1970.

Koestler, A. "The Art of Discovery and the Discoveries of Art." In: *Bricks to Babel: a Selection from 60 Years of His Writings, Chosen and with New Commentary by the Author.* New York, Random House, 1980.

Kowitz, G. T., et al. "From ERIC Source Documents to Abstracts: A Problem in Readability." Presented at the Rocky Mountain Education Research Association, Tucson, Ariz., November 29, 1973.

Kuhlen, R. "Some Similarities and Differences Between Intellectual and Machine Text Understanding for the Purpose of Abstracting." In: *Representation and Exchange of Knowledge as a Basis of Information Processes.* Edited by H. J. Dietschmann. North Holland, Neth., Elsevier Science Publishers, B. V., 1984, pp. 87–107.

Lancaster, F. W. *Indexing and Abstracting in Theory and Practice.* Champaign, Ill., University of Illinois, Graduate School of Library and Information Science, 1991.

Lancaster, F. W., and S. Herner. "Modular Content Analysis." *Proceedings of the American Documentation Institute, 27th Annual Meeting, October 1964.* Vol. 1. Washington, D.C., American Documentation Institute, 1964, pp. 403–405.

Liddy, E. D. "The Discourse-level Structure of Empirical Abstracts: An Exploratory Study." *Information Processing and Management, 27*(1):57–81, 1991.

———. "Discourse-level Structure in Abstracts." *Proceedings of the Annual Meeting of the American Society for Information Science.* Vol. 24. Medford, N.J., Learned Information, 1987, pp. 138–147.

Liddy, E. D.; S. Bonzi; J. Katzer; and E. Oddy. "A Study of Discourse Anaphora in Scientific Abstracts." *Journal of the American Society for Information Science, 38*(4):255–261, 1987.

Maizell, R. E.; J. F. Smith; and T. E. R. Singer. *Abstracting Scientific and Technical Literature: an Introductory Guide and Text for Scientists, Abstractors, and Management.* New York, Wiley-Interscience, 1971.

Manning, A. D. "Abstracts in Relation to Larger and Smaller Discourse Structures." *Journal of Technical Writing and Communication, 20*(4):369–387, 1990.

Mathis, B. A. *Techniques for the Evaluation and Improvement of Computer-Produced Abstracts.* Columbus, Ohio, Ohio State University, The Computer and Information Science Research Center, 1972. OSU-CISRC-TR-79-15

McAnulty, S. J. "Paraphrase, Summary, Precis, Advantages, Definitions, Models." *Teaching English in a Two Year College, 8*(1):47–51, 1981.

McArthur, T., ed. *The Oxford Companion to the English Language.* Oxford, Eng., Oxford University Press, 1992.

McGirr, C. J. "Guidelines for Abstracting." *Technical Communication, 5*(2): 2–5, 1978.

Mitchell, D. C. *The Process of Reading: A Cognitive Analysis of Reading and Learning to Read.* New York, Wiley, 1982.

Monsell, S. "Representations, Processes, Memory Mechanisms: The Basic Components of Cognition." *Journal of the American Society for Information Science, 32*(5):378–390, 1981.

Murray, Donald M. *The Craft of Revision.* Fort Worth, Tex., Brace Jovanovich College Publishers, 1991.

Nabokov, V. In: Pushkin, A. S. *Eugene Onegin: A Novel in Verse.* Vol. 1. Translated from the Russian. Princeton, N.J., Princeton University Press, 1981.

Nedobity, W. "The Relevance of Terminologies for Automatic Abstracting." *Journal of Information Science, 4*(4):161–165, 1982.

Nozick, Robert. *The Examined Life: Philosophical Meditations.* New York, Simon and Schuster, 1989.

Oldfield, D. E. "Document Abstracting on the Distributed Array Processor." In: *Supercomputers and Parallel Computation.* Edited by D. J. Paddon. Oxford, Eng., Oxford University Press, 1984, pp. 135–145.

Osborne, C. *W. H. Auden: The Life of a Poet.* New York, Harcourt Brace Jovanovich, 1979.

The Oxford English Dictionary. Vol. IX. 2nd ed. Prepared by J. Simpson and E. S. C. Weiner. Oxford, Eng., Clarendon Press, 1989.

Paice, C. D. "Constructing Literature Abstracts by Computer: Techniques and Prospects." *Information Processing and Management, 26*(1):171–186, 1990.

Prikhod'ko, S. M., and E. F. Skorokhod'ko. "Abstracting from Analysis of Links Between Phrases." *Nauchno-Tekhnicheskaya Informatsiya, Seriya 2, 16*(1):55–65, 1982.

Purcell, R. P. "Getting to Know LISA and Other Thoughts on Abstracting." *Library Software Review, 9*(6):357–362, 1990.

Pushkin, A. S. *Eugene Onegin: A Novel in Verse.* Vol. 1. Translated from the Russian, with a Commentary by V. Nabokov. Princeton, N.J., Princeton University Press, 1981.

Rau, L. F.; P. S. Jacobs; and U. Zernick. "Information Extraction and Text Processing Using Linguistic Knowledge Acquisition." *Information Processing and Management, 25*(4):419–428, 1989.

Rennie, D., and R. M. Glass. "Structuring Abstracts to Make Them More Informative." *Journal of the American Medical Association, 266*(1):116–117, 1991.

Root-Bernstein, R. S. "Teaching Abstracting in an Integrated Art and Science Curriculum." *Roeper Review, 13*(2):85–90, 1991.

Rowlett, R. "Sidenotes for Abstractors and Section Advisors." *CAS Report, 9*(1):8, 1980.

Rowley, J. E. *Abstracting and Indexing.* 2nd ed. London, Eng., Clive Bingley Limited, 1988.

Ruddell, R. B., and O. F. Boyle. "A Study of Cognitive Mapping as a Means to Improve Summarization and Comprehension of Expository Text." *Reading Research and Instruction, 29*(1):12–22, 1989.

Rush, J.; E. R. Salvador; and A. Zamora. "Automatic Abstracting and Indexing. Production of Indicative Abstracts by Application of Contextual Inference and Syntactic Coherence Criteria." *Journal of the American Society for Information Science, 22*(4):260–274, 1971.

Salager-Meyer, F. "Discoursal Flaws in Medical English Abstracts: A Genre Analysis per Research- and Text-type." *Text, 10*(4):365–384, 1990.

Sherrard, C. A. "The Psychology of Summary Writing." *Journal of Technical Writing and Communication, 15*(3):247–257, 1985.

Simon, H. "Information-Processing Models of Cognition." *Journal of the American Society for Information Science, 32*(5):364–377, 1981.

Sippl, Charles J., and Roger J. Sippl. *Computer Dictionary.* Indianapolis, Ind., Howard W. Sams & Co., 1984.

Smith, F. *Understanding Reading: A Psychological Analysis of Reading and Learning to Read.* 4th ed. Hillsdale, N.J., Erlbaum, 1988.

Strunk, W., and E. B. White. *The Elements of Style.* 3rd ed. New York, Macmillan Publishing, 1979.

Taylor, Robert S. *Value-Added Processes in Information Systems.* Norwood, N.J., Ablex Publishing, 1986.

Tenopir, C. "A Day in the Life of a Database Producer." *DATABASE, 15*(3):15–20, 1992.

Tenopir, C., and P. Jasco. "Quality of Abstracts." *ONLINE, 17*:44–55, May 1993.

Thistlewaite, L. L. "Summarizing: It's More than Just Finding the Main Idea." *Intervention in School and Clinic, 27*(1):25–30, 1991.

Thomas, L. *The Medusa and the Snail; More Notes of a Biology Watcher.* New York, Bantam Books, 1974.

Tibbo, H. R. "Abstracting Across the Disciplines: A Content Analysis of Abstracts from the Natural Sciences, the Social Sciences, and the Humanities with Implications for Abstracting Standards and Online Information Retrieval." *Library and Information Science Research, 14*(1):31–56, 1992.

Tichy, H. J. *Effective Writing: For Engineers, Managers, and Scientists.* New York, John Wiley & Sons, 1966.

Trawinski, B. "A Methodology for Writing Problem Structured Abstracts." *Information Processing and Management, 25*(6):693–702, 1989.

van Leunen, M.-C. *A Handbook for Scholars.* New York, Knopf, 1978.

Vaughan, D. K. "Abstracts and Summaries: Some Clarifying Distinctions." *The Technical Writing Teacher, 18*(2):132–141, 1991.

Weil B. H.; I. Zarember; and H. Owen. "Technical-Abstracting Fundamentals. I. Introduction." *Journal of Chemical Documentation, 3*(1):86–89, 1963a.

_____ . "Technical-Abstracting Fundamentals. II. Writing Principles and Practices." *Journal of Chemical Documentation, 3*(2):125–132, 1963b.

_____ . "Technical-Abstracting Fundamentals. III. Publishing Abstracts in Primary Journals." *Journal of Chemical Documentation, 3*(2):132–136, 1963c.

Woodford, F. P. "Sounder Thinking Through Clearer Writing." *Science, 156*(3776):743–745, 1967.

Zamora A., and E. M. Zamora. "Development of Natural Language Processing Systems from a Manager's Perspective." In: *Managing Artificial Intelligence and Expert Systems.* Edited by D. A. De Salvo and J. Liebowitz. Englewood Cliffs, N.J., Prentice-Hall, 1990, pp. 170–188.

Index

NOTE: This combined subject and name index includes the following features: (1) word–by–word filing of entries; (2) indented subheadings; (3) either *see* references or double entries for certain terms, whichever is deemed appropriate; (4) appendage of an asterisk to the appropriate locator page number when an individual identified in a main heading is quoted; and (5) sparse use of prepositions in subheadings.

Notes

Notes

Notes

Notes

Notes

Notes

Notes

Notes